# Modern Architecture and Expressionism

*Einstein Tower, Potsdam, 1920–1*

Dennis Sharp

# Modern Architecture and Expressionism

**George Braziller**
NEW YORK

To my wife Joanna

# Contents

# Preface

The so-called Expressionist phase of the Modern Movement in architecture is rich in fantasy, Utopian idealism and vision. It was a short-lived episode, but an inventive and effective one. The roots of Expressionism are to be found in the *Art Nouveau/Jugendstil* and in the subsequent elaboration of the implicit ideas of this style in the work of the great Individualist architects in Germany. It reached its zenith in the work of the young architects who returned from the First World War in a revolutionary frame of mind. Expressionism, in its architectural context, lasted in Germany until about 1923. In Holland the related and sympathetic 'fantastic' style of the Amsterdam School—which spanned the war years—must also be considered part of the general atmosphere of Expressionism. To one side lie the idiosyncratic works of Rudolf Steiner.

The work of the Individualists was produced during the 'womb' period of modern developments in architecture, and it seems only logical to refer to the period of Expressionism as that of the hesitant child. No one would doubt for a moment that the visionaries were playing both with ideas and paper architecture. Indeed it is this very element that has contributed to the richness of architectural form created outside the conventions of normal constructional techniques. Subsequently it was to become the main contributing factor to the death of Expressionist architecture.

The visionary period has been a 'quiet zone' for far too long. It is only over the last few years that the voices, so strong at the time, have made themselves heard again. Bruno Taut, one of the major German architects and propagandists of the twentieth century, somehow or other became lost in the shadow of the work produced by the great masters of modern architecture. Yet it was Taut who more than anyone else brought the ideas of a truly 'modern' architecture to the *avant-garde* circles of postwar Berlin and eventually to the general public through his popular books. It was Taut also who crystallized the Glass Dream of the older Expressionist poet Paul Scheerbart. Taut in his own development was an Individualist, an Expressionist (he would not have liked the title) and a Functionalist.

This book is not a history. It is rather an evaluation of an epoch through the eyes of a practising architect who has felt for a long while that the standard books on the Modern Movement in architecture have provided a distorted view.

The aim has been to explore the work of those architects who pursued a romantically orientated line in design before becoming absorbed by the Functionalist cause.

Much of the work of the Expressionist interlude (1910–23) has been looked at before, condemned and passed over. This is particularly true in such an otherwise valuable book as Sigfried Giedion's *Space, Time and Architecture* where the author brushes off the work of the Expressionist-visionary architects as 'Faustean outbursts against an inimical world. . .' He was equally wrong in his judgement that 'the Expressionist influence could not be a healthy one or perform any service to architecture' as I think time alone has proved. It is also a point that this present book seeks to refute. All art is of course concerned with expression, but it was the artists and architects who around the turn of the century saw new possibilities for their arts in terms of emotional expressiveness and spatial values. The aim of this book is to show the development of this irrational, emotional—Dionysian—approach.

Giedion was right when he wrote that 'Expressionism infiltrated all German art', and it is this fact I dwell on in the main body of the book. The fact that the Bauhaus, the seed-bed of Modern Movement ideas in design and education was staffed by Expressionist painters; that Erich Mendelsohn has had such an important influence on European architecture; that Hans Poelzig and Bruno Taut were effective leaders and spokesmen of the *Werkbund* and the *Berliner Kreis* respectively and that the Amsterdam school architecture could get so near to creating a modern 'style' of its own—admittedly while under the influence of Frank Lloyd Wright—is all-important. It is important enough I would suggest to justify this study.

Furthermore, since the mid-fifties such a change has taken place in architectural circles that now the once derisive epithets 'Expressionist' and 'Fantast' have found a new life and respectability.

Within Expressionism architecture had a very important place; it was the great banner under which all the other arts were brought together. The poet, dramatist, writer, artist and architect had a collective responsibility and each thread of artistic endeavour was linked within the total fabric of the Expressionist Movement.

In any analysis of one thread some indication must be given of the other strands, and I have at the beginning of this book briefly set out the background and aims of Expressionism. The bulk of the book is taken up with a detailed discussion of the buildings, projects and personalities within the artistic, social and political atmosphere of the period. In conclusion a short and extremely personal summary is given in an attempt to deduce an aesthetic basis for Expressionist architecture.

I have been fortunate in obtaining original documents and permissions to use copyright material that captures the contemporary spirit for the reader. Some of these documents are included in the appendices and form a link with the numerous illustrations.

A book such as this is thwarted with dangers of interpretation and explanation. It also has other limitations. It must be admitted, lastly, that in this analysis of the romantic stream in modern architecture my whole aim has been no more than to 'inscribe within a circle the polygon that comes nearest to coinciding with it'—to use a Berenson phrase. If this book rests comfortably within the circle of the Modern Movement I will be satisfied.

# Acknowledgements

This present volume has grown out of an earlier thesis submitted to Liverpool University, and I would like to acknowledge my gratitude to that University for providing me with a Leverhulme Fellowship to complete my studies during 1961–3. Since then a lot of new material has appeared on the so-called 'silent zone', and this has been incorporated in the text. I am greatly indebted to Professor Dewi-Prys Thomas for his valuable comments on the original version and to Quentin Hughes and Carl Pinfold for their continual encouragement. My thanks also go to Reyner Banham for originally suggesting this particular area of study and to the many people who have provided me with contacts, information and unpublished and out-of-print material. Of these I am particularly indebted to Kenneth Bayes of the Design Research Unit and Rex Raab for information on Rudolf Steiner; to Professor Edgar Wedepohl, Berlin; Arnold Whittick; Hans Hess; Jürgen Joedicke, Stuttgart; H. M. Wingler, Darmstadt; Professor Rookmaaker, Amsterdam; Professor Nikolaus Pevsner; Professor Julius Posener, Berlin; Professor Max Taut, Berlin; Mrs Louise Mendelsohn and Hans Schiller. My special thanks for detailed information are due to Professor Hermann Finsterlin who so kindly offered his advice and help as well as a comprehensive selection of photographs of his work.

The *Akademie der Künste*, Berlin, through the secretary of its architectural section, Peter Pfankuch, has provided many of the illustrations; Dr Ulrich Conrads of the Ullstein Verlag, Berlin, has granted permission for me to use illustrations from his *Bauwelt Fundamente* series and to quote from *Bauwelt*; Messrs Benn and Company have given permission for me to use the English translation of the text of their book on Erich Mendelsohn; *Architectura et Amicitia* have permitted me to quote from *Wendingen*— to all these my thanks are due. I am indebted also to my friends Hugo van der Wolf, Manfred Stassen and Elizabeth Burnside for help with translations and their useful comments.

Invaluable help was given by James Palmes and his staff at the RIBA Library and by Miss Enid Caldicott of the Architectural Association, London.

Arthur Korn I must thank for giving me the necessary encouragement, many years ago now, to delve into the unwritten history of the Berlin groups, and for helping me ever since. He is very largely responsible for this book taking the direction it has. The earlier thesis was dedicated to him.

To my friend Douglas Cole, who has tramped the Continent with me taking hundreds of photographs, many of which are used in this book and in the articles that it has led to in the *AA Journal* and the

*RIBA Journal*, I extend my thanks. All other photographic credits are given at the end of the book. My thanks are also extended to Christopher Newsom and Martin Marix Evans for their work in the preparation of this book and to Jeffrey Tabberner who designed it.

Finally, my last word of thanks goes to my wife who has helped so much when the pressures of practice, teaching and writing seemed almost unbearable and who has patiently checked drafts and proofs.

*Dennis Sharp*
*Manchester University*
*May 1966*

## Copyright material

We are indebted to the following for permission to reproduce copyright material:
The Managing Board of the Association 'Architectura et Amicitia' for an extract from the 'Poelzig Werkbund speech' published in *Wendingen*, No. 11, 1919; Methuen & Co. Ltd for an extract from *Dictionary of Modern Painting* edited by C. Lake and R. Maillard (originally published by Fernand Hazan Editeur, Paris), and Ullstein Verlag for 'Zur Eröffnung des Kino, "Universum"' by Erich Mendelsohn, published in *Bauwelt*, 16 October 1961 (translation by Dennis Sharp).

We would like to express our gratitude to the staffs of the Architectural Association Slide Library and the Library of the Royal Institute of British Architects for assistance in obtaining illustrations and to the following for permission to use copyright photographs, on pages mentioned:
Akademie der Künste, Berlin, 30, 35, 36, 38, 40–9, 52, 53, 56, 65, 66, 68 (right), 69, 70 (left), 71, 72, 76, 78 (including plan), 80, 86, 88, 89, 91, 92, 94, 108, 118, 120–2, 124, 128; André, Jacques, Nancy, 23, 24 (upper); The Anthroposophical Society, Dornach (Supplied by Kenneth Bayes, London), 144, 150, 152, 153, 155; Architectural Association, London, 47 (upper), 51, 57 (lower); Kenneth Bayes, 149, 164; Messrs G. Benn, 113, 115–17; Cole, Douglas, London, 24 (lower), 33, 134, 137–40, 157, 158–63; Conrads, Ulrich, Berlin, 70 (right, upper and lower), from Tant, B., *Frühlicht*, Berlin: Ullstein Verlag, 1963; F. I. Jenkins, Manchester, Frontispiece; Hermann Finsterlin, 68 (left), 98–105; National Film Archive, 57 (upper); Radio Times Hulton Picture Library, 2; Thielska Galleriet, Stockholm, 7. Other illustrations are taken from the author's own collection.

KUNST

(EXPRESSIONISTISCH)

# The roots and background of Expressionism

1

Sören Kierkegaard (1813–55). A portrait by his cousin
Christian Kierkegaard made about 1840

Friedrich Nietzsche (1844–1900)

**1**

# The Dionysian element

The emergence of Expressionism as a movement in Germany during 1910–23 indicated a revolt against tradition and accepted values. In particular it represented a distaste for neo-Romanticism which, it was generally felt, had lost touch with the reality of life and experience.

Its beginnings in the world of culture and ideas was symptomatic of later revolutions in political and social spheres. The Early Expressionist Movement acted like a warning wind before the storm of war, agitating the people to a grasp of current events. This is seen particularly in the writing and painting of the period and suggested in the designs of a number of practising German architects.

The literary origins of the Expressionist Movement are to be found in the nineteenth century, principally in the work of the German philosopher Friedrich Nietzsche (1844–1900) and the Danish Christian thinker Sören Kierkegaard (1813–55).

The new departures in Nietzsche's philosophy were concerned with a reappraisal of the Greek attitude to art and culture. In 1872 he published his revolutionary essay 'The Birth of Tragedy', which successfully challenged in terms of music and drama the current Apollonian view of art propagated in the previous century by Johann Joachim Winckelmann and Johann Wolfgang von Goethe; a view which had exemplified and yearned after 'the noble simplicity and tranquil greatness' (*Edle Einfalt und stille Grösse*) of an idealized Greece.[1] By challenging this ideal Nietzsche emphasized not the expression of conscious self-control in Greek art but its very antithesis, the elements of fate and desperation—in other words the Dionysian aspects.

As Oscar Levy has written, 'Nietzsche looked forward to the human race emerging from the effete culture of tradition, and re-establishing itself, on a basis in harmony with man's primitive instincts'.[2]

The idea that art was merely concerned with external beauty was thus at variance with Nietzsche's views, as indeed it was with the ideas of the later Expressionists.

Samuel and Thomas in their important book, *Expressionism in German Art, Life, Literature and the Theatre*, noted that 'the terms in which Expressionists speak of their "*Weltanschauung*" resemble closely the manner in which Nietzsche speaks of Greece', and point out the debt that such Expressionist apologists

3

as Wilhelm Michel owe to Nietzsche's writings.[3] 'Everything in the world of antiquity', says Michel, 'was dynamic. The God invaded life profoundly and with the strength of a storm. Hence the possibility of the great tragic form in poetry and the splendid development of Man in the face of an overwhelming Fate.'[4]

Nietzsche in his essay presents artistic creation as a wild intoxication—*Rausch*: 'Overwhelmed, stunned and inspired by an explosion of his vital energies, the artist becomes possessed with Dionysian madness; the "eternal lust for becoming" breaks forth.'[5]

The essay 'The Birth of Tragedy' is concerned with music and dramatic art in which Dionysian enchantment is the important factor, and Nietzsche indicates that 'In this enchantment the Dionysian reveller sees himself as a satyr, and as a satyr he in turn beholds the god that is, in his transformation he sees a new vision outside himself as the Apollonian consummation of his state. With this new vision the drama is complete.'[6]

It can be clearly seen from this why a philosophy which took such a subjective interpretation of the past and which also emphasized and externalized emotional states could easily be accepted in the chaotic years up to the time of the First World War. With his Dionysian idea of a more dynamic view of the artist's role in society Nietzsche combined the concept of the Superman; a Superman who would fight against the Naturalism and Neo-Romanticism found in nineteenth-century art and drama. Nietzsche himself fought these tendencies and also exposed art, religion, and philosophy 'as illusions invented by man . . . in his struggle for development'.[7]

Nietzsche maintained that it is only when the good, the true and the beautiful becomes useful to the individual, that the Superman is established. The Superman has victory over others by his belief in himself as a person of both spiritual and creative power. For Nietzsche the spiritual and creative qualities in man were one; not in seeking a personal God in the Christian sense, but in producing great works of art as an expression of life.

Nietzsche was in fact proposing a sensuous theory of art, 'a stimulating of animal energies by images and desires of an enhanced life'.[8] He is quoted as saying: 'I agree with the artists more than with all philosophers up to now: they did not lose the great track where life advances, they were fond of the things of "this world"—they were fond of their senses.'[9]

It was Kasimir Edschmid, the chief Expressionist apologist, who elaborated Nietzsche's theories and claimed 'that existence should consist of "perpetual excitement" and that the artist's work should be "the outburst of his (the artist's) inner self"'.[10]

This perpetual excitement suggested by Edschmid is really another way of expressing the idea of artistic inspiration. And it is on this very aspect of creativity that Nietzsche made an important contribution.

In looking back on the writing of *Also Sprach Zarathustra* Nietzsche, in his last work produced before he died, *Ecce Homo*, tells of his own creative experience between the years 1883 and 1885, when he was struggling with the themes of what is probably his best known work.[11]

His personal *Rausch* with the emotional and creative problems set by the work is presented clearly in

4

the following extract, which stands by itself as a moving analysis of the processes of artistic activity. 'Has anyone,' he wrote, 'at the end of the nineteenth century any distinct notion of what poets of a stronger age understood by the word inspiration? If not, I will describe it. If one had the slightest trace of superstition left in one, it would hardly be possible to set aside the idea that one is the incarnation, mouthpiece, and medium of almighty powers. The idea of revelation, in the sense that something suddenly and with unspeakable certainty and purity becomes visible, audible, something that profoundly convulses and upsets one, simply describes the fact. One hears—one does not seek; One takes—one does not ask who gives; a thought suddenly flashes up like lightning, it comes of necessity and unfalteringly formed—I have never had a choice in the matter. One is seized by an ecstasy, whose fearful tension is sometimes relieved in a storm of tears, while one's steps now involuntarily rush along, now involuntarily lag. . . .

Everything is in the highest degree involuntary, but takes place as if in a tempest of freedom, of absoluteness, of power and divinity. The involuntary nature of the figures and similes is the most remarkable thing; one no longer has any conception of what is imagery, what metaphor; everything presents itself in the readiest, the truest and simplest means of expression. . . This is *my* experience of inspiration.'[12]

Although Nietzsche claimed that one would probably have to go back thousands of years to find a similar experience it would not seem too presumptuous to look for similar creative moments in the work of the Expressionist writers and artists of this century. For them, as George Grosz wrote in his book, *A little yes and a big no*, 'the expression of one's inner self was all that mattered'.[13]

Sören Kierkegaard's works, which were published in Denmark in the middle of the nineteenth century, were not translated into German until the end of the first decade of the twentieth century, although a book had been written in German on his philosophy by Höffding in 1896.[14] Kierkegaard's contribution to Expressionist ideas has largely been through his questioning and analytical writings and through his self-imposed idea of genius.

In Germany Kierkegaard's religious, aesthetic and ethical ideas were appreciated by such Existentialist thinkers as Buber, Jaspers and Heidegger, as well as by fringe Expressionists like the Prague-born Franz Kafka, and his friend Max Brod.[15] In fact Kafka's own life seems to have been fatalistically modelled on that of Kierkegaard; each of these brilliant men had heart-breaking love affairs which seriously affected their work, both sought in vain for God and the reality of the religious experience, both used a literary style that had a strange indirectness and both tragically died at an early age, Kierkegaard when he was forty-two and Kafka when he was forty-one.

In his novels *The Trial*, *The Castle*, and *America* (known as the 'trilogy of despair') Franz Kafka caught the real background of the Expressionist Movement, with its reflection of material instability, spiritual searching and an overriding feeling of despair. Kafka presented subjectively a new vision, a reality in which the individual was inextricably caught, held and cornered.

An undercurrent of discontent and unhappiness is characteristic of Expressionist literature and drama, and although in later years there appears to have been a longing for a vision that could come to terms with contemporary society it was this emotional suffering that weakened the Expressionists' position. This weakness is evident even in the early 'dream plays' of the Swedish dramatist August Strindberg (1849–1912) who had a powerful influence on many of the German Expressionists. Indeed, as Samuel and Thomas point out in their book 'there can be found in Strindberg's work nearly all the characteristics of Expressionism. His influence can be measured from the fact that in the years 1913–15 more than a thousand performances of his plays were given in sixty-two German cities.'[16]

However, his importance must not be summed up just in terms of numbers such as these, but rather in the fact that Strindberg, whose Nordic pietistic sensibility found its best expression in complicated visionary dramas saw the hopeless situation of mankind. It was a situation in which man was constantly at the mercy of fate or daemonic powers. Out of this dilemma Strindberg created a patriarchal system of society in which the female was 'assigned a tragic intermediate position between the powers of good and evil; she is a figure of light or a daemon, often both'.[17]

In common with his contemporary the Norwegian painter, Edvard Munch (1863–1944), whom he first met in Berlin in the last decade of the nineteenth century, Strindberg probed the wounds of human emotions and despair: '. . . he opened up new depths of irrational experience, new horizons beyond the pale of reality, and in fact Strindberg's doctrine of suffering was given an active turn by the Expressionists who proclaimed suffering as essential for the victory of the New Man.'[18]

Strindberg's significance as a primary influence on Expressionist dramatists is obvious, but the fact that he was also a mature painter has often been overlooked. He began painting as early as the 1870s although it was not until the mid-1890s that he became absorbed with the painterly task of trying to express spontaneously, often in abstract terms, experience and emotion through colour and form. He has been quoted as saying:

'I approach my painting with only a vague idea of what I want to present. With my spatula, I throw on colours, distributing them and mixing them right on the surface. I am mixing many colours, fourteen,

*Friedrich Nietzsche. A portrait by Edvard Munch*

fifteen perhaps, evolving a labyrinth of hues and shapes. Finally, the entire surface is swimming in colour. I step back to look at my work and I can't explain what it may mean.'[19]

In contrast to his hesitancy about the meaning of his paintings, Strindberg had very clear ideas about his plays. He explained in a lucid Preface to what is often held to be his best work, *A Dream Play*, the complications of reproducing 'the detached and disunited—although apparently logical—form of dreams'. In pure Expressionist prose he wrote in explanation:

'Anything is apt to happen, anything seems possible and probable. Time and space do not exist. On a flimsy foundation of actual happenings, imagination spins and weaves in new patterns: an intermingling of remembrances, experiences, whims, fancies, ideas, fantastic absurdities and improvisations, and original inventions of the mind. The personalities split, take on duality, multiply, vanish, intensify, diffuse and disperse, and are brought into a focus. There is, however, one single-minded consciousness that exercises a dominance over the characters: the dreamer's.'[20]

It is the dreamer's world with which this present study is concerned. A world in which man is shown attempting to come to terms with the new knowledge and developments at his disposal. The dream occurred at a period in time when architects, artists and writers sought inspiration through their own experience and activity in an attempt to solve problems that had not been attempted before. The effects of war and the rumours of war can be held largely responsible for the attitude of mind at the time but each artist involved in the Dionysian madness must be held responsible for his own particular vision.

*August Strindberg. A woodcut by Edvard Munch*

# 2

# A period of conflict and vision

As a series of separate states, Germany had been involved in mounting territorial conflicts since the time of Napoleon. After its late consolidation as a single power a new and more provocative militarism arose. Eventually a three-fold policy developed that welded this latent militarism to progressive industry and to a gestating yet virile art movement. This resulted in a serious break within the various parts of society on political grounds and paradoxically a closer alliance of industry, art and commerce; an alliance which saw the independent designer brought into the service of the progressive industrialists and the creation, largely due to the enthusiasm of Hermann Muthesius, of the *Deutscher Werkbund* in 1907. The commercial and industrial leaders were called to the service of the nation to help the Kaiser in his ambition to gain control of the Seven Seas. The Kaiser himself was a reactionary, who forced his imperialistic attitude on the nation. The Kaiser's political views led inevitably to Germany finding herself without a single friend left in the world except Austria.

After the precipitation of the Bosnian Crisis in June 1914, when the heir to the Austrian throne, the Archduke Ferdinand, was shot at Sarajevo, the massacre began. The 'war to end all wars' left Europe stunned by the intensity of battle and the absurdity of international politics and intrigue. It caused an abrupt end to all activity in the arts and in building.

After the battle came the lull; a period of intense depression for victor and loser alike when the most terrible economic and social hardships were experienced.

Internally Germany was completely disorganized. Civil wars caused political unrest and a search began for radical ideas for a renewed society. The socialists found themselves in power and demanded a society based on revolutionary principles of government and social organization.

The communists, and many of the socialists too, had admired the changes made in Russia after the Revolution and they looked to a similar social revolution, but without bloodshed, in their own country. Although a communist revolt did in fact take place in the Ruhr in 1920, the Weimar Constitution afforded a compromise between the views of the different parties and the unrest was checked for a time at least. It was in this atmosphere of postwar disintegration and despair that a search for a deeper and

9

*Title page. Franz Pfemfert's Aktion*

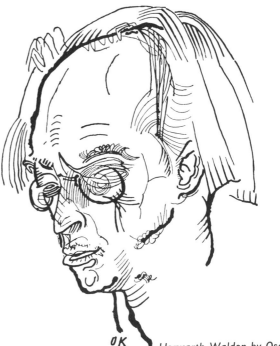

*Herwarth Walden by Oscar Kokoschka*

more personal expression in the arts took place. There was no question now whether the probative ideas put forward before the war under the banner of Expressionism had any validity; they obviously had. The German nation was at the height of its emotional state in the years 1918 to 1920 and the influence of the early Expressionists' work only added creative fire to this state. In the postwar period there was a ready acceptance of the ideas that had their roots in the philosophic concepts of Nietzsche and Kierkegaard, in the plays of August Strindberg, in the paintings of the Fauves and Edvard Munch, and in the architecture of National Romanticism and *Art Nouveau*. The exploratory nature of the ideas inherent in the designs of the prewar period now took on a new reality and became the obsessive concern of the younger architects. They became the fabric of the Utopian dream.

It is almost impossible to fix a firm date to the beginnings of any art movement. Historically every manifestation of a new trend in art presumes at least a formative period of currency. This was so with Expressionism.

By 1910 the emergent Expressionist Movement had gained identity. It should be remembered though that it was much earlier, in 1905, that the 'Expressionist' painter, Karl Schmidt-Rottluff, one of the founder members of the *Brücke* group at Dresden, spoke of the attempt 'to attract all revolutionary and fermenting elements' to the group.[1] While the members of the New Artists Federation, *Neue Künstler Vereinigung* at Munich, out of which the *Blaue Reiter* group was formed, began to grapple in earnest with new problems in painting around 1909. Thus any kind of dating can only be approximate.

10

In 1910–11 the Expressionist Movement had become strong enough to support two periodicals, *Der Sturm*, the mouthpiece of Herwarth Walden's Berlin Gallery of the same name and *Die Aktion*, a literary magazine, edited by Franz Pfemfert. The titles were significant, descriptive nouns that set the seal on the revolutionary spirit—the violent disturbance of the tempest or storm; action, the exertion of energy.

Certainly Expressionism proved to be both a disturbing and energetic episode, a Dionysian trait in a predominantly revolutionary *milieu*, both the prophecy and product of the débâcle of a nation. As well as this it was an art and literary movement that brought together some of the finest and most creative minds of the twentieth century. The Expressionist Movement was a vast melting-pot for new ideas and experiments. Expressionism was revolution in art. In its wider application it was revolution in life also, an attempt to re-establish the unity of experience; that of the individual in society.

The actual term 'Expressionism' was it seems first introduced by a French painter, Julien-Auguste Hervé, as early as 1901. He exhibited eight paintings that year in the *Salon des Indépendants* in Paris to which he gave the title '*expressionismes*'. However, it was not until a few years later that the term itself began to appear in Germany. Again it was used as a description of paintings. Wilhelm Worringer, the art historian and theorist, wrote in Walden's magazine *Der Sturm* about the 'Parisian Synthetists and Expressionists, Cézanne, Van Gogh and Matisse'.[2] It should be remembered that as early as 1878 Cézanne had described the art of painting as a '*moyen d'expression de sensation*'.[3] Soon after 1910 the term became widely applied to all work that showed what were called 'anti-Impressionist traits'; work that was both by and in the style of the Fauves. Werner Haftmann, for example, has said that the *Neue Künstler Vereinigung* in Munich 'shows us the situation in 1910—the organic transformation of the Jugendstil into Fauvism which in its German version may with a slight change of emphasis be termed "Early Expressionism".'[4]

Gradually the term 'Expressionism' spread from painting to include literature, drama, music and eventually architecture.

In literature the term 'Expressionist' was first used by critics to describe the style of Kasimir Edschmid's collected stories *Die sechs Mündungen* of 1915, although as Samuel and Thomas point out Edschmid claims he 'himself had never heard of the term'.[5] From this it can be seen that the use of the term was rather vague and it is helpful for this present study to find in the *Concise Oxford dictionary* a definition which reflects reasonably accurately the contemporary usage. Expressionism is defined as the 'Modern tendency among painters, dramatic authors etc., to subordinate realism to the symbolic or stylistic expression of the artist's or character's inner experience. . . .'[6]

This definition is given more precision if we add to 'inner experience' the word 'meaning'. Then we come close to the real aim of the Expressionists. For not only were the artists and writers interested in the varieties of personal experience and in the externalization of their own feelings but also in the inner, suggested meaning of inanimate objects.

'A house,' wrote Edschmid, 'is no longer merely a subject for an artist, consisting of stone, ugly or beautiful; it has to be looked at until its true form has been recognized, until it is liberated from the muffled restraint of a false reality, until everything that is latent within it is expressed.'[7]

Another useful definition of Expressionism is given in *A dictionary of modern painting*, which states that it 'denotes a permanent tendency in art, characteristic of the Nordic countries, which becomes accentuated in times of social stress or spiritual disturbance. Expressionism has found particularly fertile soil for expansion in our turbulent age. Although the idea always existed, the term for it is a recent invention of German aesthetics, popularized by Herwarth Walden, publisher of the *avant-garde* review *Der Sturm*, in Berlin, who classified under the heading of Expressionism—as opposed to Impressionism— all the revolutionary manifestations between 1910 and 1920, including Cubism and the abstract trends. This broad definition, as confused as it is exaggerated, is to be found in the writings of nearly all those who concerned themselves with Expressionism. . . . There are two conflicting viewpoints—the one putting the accent on "plastic form" and its autonomy, the other on psychological "force" and its impetus—bringing up again the traditional duality of Classicism and Romanticism, of being and becoming, of the Latin and German temperaments. Expressionism constitutes the present phase of Romanticism, in a tragic mode, bound to the anguish of our times. . . . Expressionism favoured individual and ethnic distinctions.'[8]

It can be seen that although the art of the Nordic countries has at times of national strife and social upheaval always produced an expressive art form, the distinctive nature of the works of art produced during the years 1910–23 was due to the fact that they were bound up with what Lothar Schreyer has called 'the spiritual movement of a time that places inner experience above external life'.[9]

Two of the key concepts within the movement of Expressionism were Vision and Utopia. The Expressionists felt themselves to be true visionaries and Edschmid defines them in his manifesto thus:

'They did not look,
They envisioned,
They did not photograph,
They had visions.
Instead of the rocket, they created the
perpetual state of excitement.'[10]

Expressionism constitutes the twentieth-century basis of Romanticism. Its Dionysian origins, its irrationalism and morbid concern with emotional problems were but a reflection of the anguish of the times.

The new view superseded the inadequate notions of the Symbolists, and the curvilinear Naturalism that had pervaded the *Jugendstil*, and brought about a marriage of the spiritual and the individualistic. It put man at the centre; from there he was to transform the world to his own new visionary plan.[11] The spiritual element however was not confined to a concept of man's creative power. The phenomenal rise in the number of religious and semi-religious sects and cults can also be attributed to man's renewed

Zeichnung von Oskar Kokoschka zu dem Drama
**Mörder, Hoffnung der Frauen**

spiritual awareness. Of the many sects prevalent in Germany during the twenties Rudolf Steiner's Anthroposophical Movement is of particular importance because of its close relationship to the architecture of Expressionism.

### The international aspects of expressionism

Expressionism must not be considered an isolated phenomenon. The times were full of often less important but equally novel and fashionable 'isms'. In their book *The isms of art*, published in 1925, El Lissitzky and Hans Arp attempted an examination of the whole complexity of art up to that time. The photographic catalogue of art styles covered work in fourteen different countries and read backwards from 1924 to 1914, commencing with Abstract Film and ending with Expressionism. This slim volume provides a useful summary of the trends in art circles, which can only be understood if one realizes that each of the stylistic manifestations had its own innovator (e.g. El Lissitzky's own invention of the painterly concept 'Proun', in 1920), apologists and fanatical supporters.

The relative importance of single movements within the general surfeit can now be seen more objectively and it is questionable whether the verdict of Lissitzky and Arp on Expressionism has any real validity. 'From cubism and futurism has been chopped the minced meat, the mystic German beefsteak: expressionism.'

In outlook the Expressionist Movement was essentially European. It was not just an aesthetic tendency rooted in a single nation. '*Sie ist Übernational*', proclaimed Edschmid, a '*Forderung des Geistes . . . eine Frage der Seele, ein Ding der Menschheit.*'

It has been said that Expressionism was a 'European tendency firmly rooted in the condition of the age, on which it provides an invaluable commentary'.[12] In revolutionary zeal and spirit it corresponded to the Futurism of Marinetti and his circle in Paris and Italy, whose demand was for a new ideal of beauty based on the modern concepts of speed and motion. 'A racing car . . . is more beautiful than the Winged Victory of Samothrace', the Foundation Manifesto of Futurism declared in 1909.[13] It is not surprising therefore to find that in 1912 the Futurists held an exhibition in Herwarth Walden's *Der Sturm* gallery in Berlin and the dynamic paintings of Boccioni and the work of other Futurists were seen at first hand. A year earlier the Futurist Manifesto had appeared in Walden's *Der Sturm* magazine. The Futurists like the Expressionists demanded a distinct break with tradition 'and the creation of a "dynamic experience" as an end in itself'.[14]

In England, besides the activity of E. Gordon Craig and the revolution he started in stage design, the 'Imagist Manifesto' had appeared in 1913, in which an aesthetic doctrine was outlined that came close to the literary ideas of the German Expressionist writers.[15] Soon after this Wyndham Lewis produced the first issue of his periodical *Blast* and acknowledged the debt owed by all the international 'modern movement' manifestos to Germany.[16] Quite clearly also elements corresponding to Expressionism are to be detected in the writings of T. S. Eliot and James Joyce, although they certainly were not identical with it, as Samuel and Thomas point out: 'It must not be forgotten that a comparison of Expressionism with the modernist spirit in English literature involves a question of parallelism rather than of identity.'[17]

*Expressionism and the young*

Expressionism, like its predecessor the *Jugendstil*, was a youthful movement; a movement in which the young felt they had a mission of deliverance to accomplish. Ernst Wilhelm Lotz in his book of 1913, *The setting out of youth*, declared their messianic mission:

'Radiant by the morning, we are the enlightened. Our youthful heads are surmounted by the apices of Messiah crowns. Gleaming new worlds spring from our foreheads, fulfilment and the future, days above which a flag heralds the coming storm'.

The mission was to bring the new generation out from the arid deserts of superficial Naturalism to a land of new values and independence. 'We want to whip up Naturalism to fanatic vision', declared Edschmid in his essay on the young German poets.

The literature of the time contains many violent and vociferous attacks on the older generation; they were blamed for the sufferings and failings of the young. Such attacks often took the form of personalized dramatic works or poems. A typical example of this tendency and probably the most famous of the so-called 'Ich-dramas' was Reinhard Johannes Sorge's Der Bettler. This presents autobiographically the bitter struggle of parent and child. It declares a personal distrust in the older generation as well as a distrust in the confines of earthly reality. The underlying theme of the drama, which owes much to the concepts of Nietzsche, is 'the destruction of the narrowing barriers of an earthbound reality and the establishment of life upon a wider and more imaginative basis, whereon a new and greater type of man will grow up and thrive'.[18]

It has been stressed earlier in this chapter that the feeling and background of the movement was one of material instability, spiritual searching and an overriding feeling of despair, and it is this emotional characteristic that is to be found in much of the work produced by the painters, writers, dramatists, sculptors and architects of the time. In painting this can best be observed in the work of Ernst Ludwig Kirchner (1880–1938); Franz Marc (1880–1916); Wassily Kandinsky (1866–1944); Emil Nolde (1867–1956) and Oscar Kokoschka (born 1886). The latter, although not exactly an Expressionist in the full meaning of the word, was actively engaged in Walden's Sturm circle and through his essentially individualistic vision reflected better than any other artist the confusion of the age. In sculpture the powerful, almost medieval forms used by Ernst Barlach (1870–1938) took on a political slant, and he used his work to evoke an emotional response to the position of the poor and the peasant. The study by Bernard S. Myers of Expressionist painting, Expressionism: a generation in revolt, gives a completely objective appraisal of the aims and achievements of each of these artists both inside the various groups and as individuals.

The creative lead in literature and drama was given by writers such as George Kaiser (1878–1945), whose play The Burghers of Calais (1914) caused something of a sensation during the war years; Franz Werfel (1890–1945); Kasimir Edschmid (born 1890); Gottfried Benn (1886–1956); Walter Hasenclever (1890–1940) and Franz Kafka (1883–1924). Again it is the last-named fringe-Expressionist who is probably best known outside German speaking circles today for his attempt through his writing to come to terms with the despair and inevitability of the human situation. Ernst Barlach and Oscar Kokoschka were also among the pioneers of Expressionist drama and their published works demonstrate how close the ties were between the Expressionism of the practising artists and the writers. In Barlach's case particularly drama was as important a medium as sculpture—and he excelled in both. In point of fact the overlapping of the work of the artists and writers is so complex at times that one must view the Expressionist Movement as a whole rather than attempt a too rigid compartition.

*The basis of Expressionist art*

Expressionism in painting, Erich Mendelsohn wrote, 'represents a new form of an emotional conception of life leading to artistic revolution. The inner expression became more important than the impression of the outer world'.[19]

The Expressionist painter founded his concept on the basis of a subjective interpretation of reality. In the early stages of Expressionist development it was the expression on canvas or in sculpture of emotional states and concepts that was of primary importance. Thus the art of the Expressionist phase was not merely descriptive or representational but rather analytical and subjective, leading inevitably to the abstraction of subject matter.

Such an introspective view of the facts of reality and experience as that presented by the Expressionists was in no way new to the Nordic sensibility. The elements of suffering and despair have a definite place in the artistic history of the Germanic people. It has been suggested—by Herbert Read—that the whole of the Gothic North can lay claim to standards that 'constitute a tradition equal and opposite . . . to the Latin tradition, and one which, if we could discount the effects of acquired culture, would have a more natural appeal to northern races'.[20]

It is certainly true that many parallels are to be found in the work of modern Expressionist artists with their own past, a past that reached its own artistic heights in the paintings and drawings of Albrecht Dürer, Matthias Grünewald, Hans Holbein and the Cranachs, and in the sculpture of Tilman Riemenschneider and Viet Stoss. The Isenheim Alterpiece by Grünewald (now in the Museum Unterlinden, Colmar), with its 'crassly realistic pictures expressed in a cruel stark language' was particularly important to the German Expressionist artists.[21]

It can be said that Expressionism revived the emotional and spiritual elements in art, and placed man's experience of the world at the centre. It was a reaction to Impressionism which had advocated the close identification of colour with nature. Some of the Expressionist painters sought to introduce a new symbolism of colour that was associated with the mood of the painting; red for passion, blue for love, white for innocence and so on. The colours themselves were applied liberally on the canvas; vivid, and often unmixed. Kandinsky in his book *Concerning the spiritual in art* makes a long analysis of the associative theories of colour, in which he compares painting with harmony. A relationship of music and colour harmony had been outlined earlier by Goethe, and these views were further developed by the founder of Anthroposophy, Rudolf Steiner. Steiner sought to extend Goethe's treatises on colour into a complete creative vocabulary. He, like Kandinsky, saw the importance of the relation of colour to form and subsequently elaborated a theory of art that took these two aspects as the most important elements in art.

Edvard Munch, the Norwegian painter, is often referred to as the most important influence on Expressionist painting, embodying in his work an emotional intensity that was without precedent in European circles at the time. Munch was interested in subjects which held an intense dramatic value. He was a psychiatrist whose subjects were analysed on canvas and not on the couch.

16

Munch's art was distinguished from the current romanticism and Impressionism by its very intensity—with themes that were simple, yet frank and poignant studies of deep emotional problems. By his style, or seeming lack of style, the observer is held on the brink of a personal crisis. The dramatic value of the situations he recorded were indicated in the titles he gave to various paintings and drawings—titles like 'The Cry', 'The Dead Mother', 'The Sick Child', 'Puberty', etc. Single subjects like these, Munch dealt with in brevity of line and vivid colours. Although the portrayal of human emotions and human situations was of primary importance to him, he did not ignore the painterly problems of light and shade, texture, composition or for that matter, stylization. And it was these elements too that interested the later German Expressionist painters. However, it is the sacred element in art—the spiritual—that concerned Munch and he recorded in his diary his attitude to painting the joys and sorrows of life: 'No more painting of interiors with women knitting and men reading. I want to bring home to the spectator the sacred element in all human beings so that he takes off his hat to them as he would in church.'

As early as 1900 Ernst Ludwig Kirchner claims he had the 'audacious idea of revitalising German art. 'Indeed I did, and the impulse came to me while looking at an exhibition of the Munich Secessionists . . . indoors were hung these anaemic, bloodless, lifeless studio daubs. Outside was life, noisy and colourful, pulsating. . . .

'First of all I tried to find a method whereby I could seize the effect of motion . . . how to arrest movement in a few bold strokes, catching the passing moment and finding new forms. . . .

'My sense of design was simplified and strengthened by the fact that I had learned to make wood-cuts from my father when I was only 15 years old. So armed, I arrived in Dresden and during my studies there I was able to arouse my friends' enthusiasm over my new ideas.

'My goal was always to express emotion and experience with large and simple forms and clear colours.'[22] The above extracts are a particularly explicit account of the aims and history of the Dresden *Die Brücke* group. Discontent with the Academy; the bold attempt to create new forms with an economy of line; the woodcut; the emphasis on the emotional content of art; all these factors added up to the first manifestation of what is now termed German Expressionist painting. The *Brücke* group was founded in 1905 by Fritz Bleyl (whom Kirchner had met in 1902), Kirchner himself, Erich Heckel and Karl Schmidt-Rottluff. Its formation was, as Peter Selz has written 'one of the most revolutionary events in the history of modern painting'.[23]

A significant fact about the members of the *Brücke* group was that both Kirchner and Heckel had studied architecture at Dresden, and this is reflected in the architectonic forms used in much of their work. The artists of *Die Brücke* made an intuitive search for a new expression in art and to this end developed an interest in Negro art and in primitive German art. The etchings, lithographs and woodcuts made by the members of the Dresden group are among the finest works to have come out of the Expressionist movement.

Emile Nolde joined the *Brücke* group for a short period in 1906 and brought his extremely personal attitude to colour, as well as his highly personal style of fantasy to an already diverse group. Otto Mueller (1874–1930), a painter who was passionately interested in gipsy and circus themes, joined the *Brücke* in 1910, but already by that date, after the group had moved to Berlin, the bridge itself was beginning to crack. Finally in 1913, after the publication of the *Chronicle of the Brücke*, it collapsed. The *Brücke* group had spanned the years from Fauvism to the beginnings of the new revolutionary movement of *Der Blaue Reiter* (The Blue Horseman), which began in Munich under the inspiration of Wassily Kandinsky. It was on 18 December 1911 that the first of the *Blaue Reiter* exhibitions was opened at the Thannhauser Gallery. In 1911 Kandinsky led a group of artists away from the *Neue Künstler Vereinigung* (N.K.V.) over a matter of principle even though the Association had been created to further experimental ideas in art and had been founded in 1909 at Munich under Kandinsky's leadership. Kandinsky seceded from the Association with Münter, Kubin and Franz Marc. It was a secession that was necessary, as so few of the people within the Artists' Association shared Kandinsky's enthusiasm for non-figurative painting. The direction of the new group was largely in the hands of Kandinsky's young disciple Franz Marc. The new group called themselves *Der Blaue Reiter*; a name that came from the title of one of Kandinsky's own paintings of 1903. Much later, in 1924, after Klee, Jawlensky and Feininger had joined Kandinsky (Marc had been killed at Verdun in 1916) another group was formed called the Blue Four (*Die Blaue Vier*). Within the *Blaue Reiter* group Kandinsky developed his ideas for a non-figurative type of painting. Kandinsky was concerned with what he termed the 'inner necessity' of a picture. 'The most important thing about form, is to know whether or not it emerges from an inner necessity.'[24] With his exploration of the world of form in his early paintings a basis was provided for the whole development of the twentieth-century form of art that is termed 'abstract expressionist'. In his first major treatise *Concerning the spiritual in art*, written in 1910 and published in 1912, Kandinsky had given an outline of his ideas. By 1925 he was able to formulate clearly these ideas in his *Point and line to plane*. This book, produced after he had begun teaching at the Bauhaus, presented as Carola Giedion-Welcker has said:

'. . . a new formal theory of the elements of drawing, the base of which, however, is always the same notion of the "irrational and mystical" spiritual unity. "Modern art can be born only where signs become symbols". Point and line are here detached from all explanatory and utilitarian purpose and transposed to the realm of the a-logical. They are advanced to the rank of autonomous, expressive essences, as colours had been earlier.'[25]

In 1922 Kandinsky had moved to the *Bauhaus* at Weimar where he joined in the new school's art teaching activities with Paul Klee and Lyonel Feininger. These painters created what Walter Gropius has called the 'spiritual counterpoint' of the place and through their efforts brought much closer to reality the idea of a *Zukunftskathedrale*. But this attempt was cut short by a number of factors not the least of which was the new emphasis on the *Wohnmaschine*. The eventual split, caused by many differences of policy and ideas among the staff after the move to Dresden, occurred in 1928 when Hannes Meyer took over the directorship from Gropius.

18

# Architecture and Expressionism

2

# 3

# The basis of Expressionist architecture

In the general movement of Expressionism in Germany (1910–23) architecture only played a peripheral role. Even so, it was through the revolutionary cultural atmosphere of the Expressionist Movement that an impetus was given to a more personal and emotional search for solutions to architectural problems. Forms were exaggerated and stylized, Utopian concepts developed, and in the work of a number of architects emphasis was placed on monumentalism, symbolism and on what seemed at first glance to be a 'new irrationality'.

No distinct 'Expressionist' school of architects ever existed as such; the use of the terms 'Expressionist' and 'Expressionism' to describe certain tendencies in the work of individual architects and groups is largely retrospective. The terms have now become definitive through their constant use by architectural critics and historians and the epithets 'visionary', 'fantastic', 'dream' and 'Utopian architecture', which were often used in the immediate postwar period, have been largely replaced by this single blanket term 'Expressionism'. In many ways this is a useful, although often misleading classification, as it under-lines the close correspondence between the aims and ideals of the *littérateurs*, dramatists, painters, sculptors and architects of the period. Indeed, as Sigfried Giedion has pointed out 'Expressionism infiltrated all German art', touching 'almost every German worker in the arts'.

The roots of this so-called Expressionist architecture are to be found in two nineteenth-century stylistic movements: National Romanticism and *Art Nouveau.*

Vittorio Gregotti has summed it up in this way:

'In speaking of expressionism in architecture, one important point should be kept in mind: that it derived its own vocabulary directly from the deformation of the romantic-nationalistic architecture of the turn of the century. Linked as it was to the neo-Romantic architecture in most European countries, romantic-nationalistic architecture was certainly one of the most widespread phenomena, along with Art Nouveau, present in architecture at the end of the nineteenth century, one of the most serious attempts to break away from eclecticism. Germany, Holland, Scandinavia, Finland and Italy were all influenced in one way or another. And it is not by chance that these are the nations which had most recently (with respect to Austria, England, France and Spain) satisfied their aspirations to national unity.'[1] The external character and internal shaping of many of the National Romantic and *Art Nouveau* buildings suggested a kind of architecture that would emerge when it was finally freed from stylistic overtones and wilful eclecticism. The dynamic, yet somewhat exploratory designs of architects such as Victor Horta in Brussels, Eugène Vallin and Emile André in Nancy, Hector Guimard in Paris, Antonio Gaudí in Barcelona, the work of the 'Glasgow Four' and the Sezessionists in Vienna provided a number of inspirational starting points for the later radical Expressionists. While it was the work of Henri van de Velde, Peter Behrens and August Endell that successfully bridged the gap between nineteenth-century eclecticism and twentieth-century modernism.

It would be too perverse to suggest that Expressionist architecture grew directly from these two nineteenth-century movements; it is rather that these styles were part of what P. Morton Shand has referred to as 'that hyper-aesthetic *maladie de la fin du siècle*', which produced its own revolutionary atmosphere in which artists, designers and architects considered the work they carried out both original and 'Modern'.

The newness was indicated by a concern with structural rationalization, with new forms of decoration (both internal and façade decoration), with the problems of the expressive role of architectural form and ornamentation, and to a limited extent with monumentalism. However, with the architectural ideas current at the end of the nineteenth century there was still a distinct lack of stylistic coherence, as indeed there was in the other aesthetic movements such as Symbolism, Synthetism, the Nabis, and even Fauvism, all of which extended their influence well into the new century. Stylistic coherence only came with the essentially twentieth-century ideas embodied in Cubism, Futurism, Expressionism, Neo-plasticism and Abstract art. It was these movements that translated into art terms the twentieth-century ideas of the machine, speed and movement, the psychological awareness of space, and communication.

In Germany the beginnings of an Expressionistic architecture, as distinct from the mere extension of *Art Nouveau/Jugendstil* ideas, are to be found in the very original work of Hans Poelzig as early as 1908. He, together with other Individualistic architects such as van de Velde and Peter Behrens represented the prewar exploratory phase of Early Expressionist architecture which was of such emotional significance to the later and younger postwar visionaries. The war provided a break between the work of the Individualistic architects and the postwar phase of visionary architecture; it was an artificial break in which all building activity ceased and labour was directed to the more urgent task of producing material for war. During this period convincing ideas on the future of architecture emerged but quite naturally these were confined to paper.

After the war had ended the architectural position had changed, young men emerged from the holocaust eager to rebuild the world and the pioneer Individualists were looked upon as the protagonists of the new movement. A number of these men, who had pioneered the way for a new architecture, gained high executive positions as city architects and educationalists as well as important commissions. Poelzig, Behrens and Taut straddled the gap of the war years with consummate ease, although a great change can

*The Vaxelaire shopfront, Nancy, 1902. Entrance door detail.*
*Architects: Emile Andre in collaboration with Vallin*

The main frontage of the
Vaxelaire shop

Josef Maria Olbrich: Ernst
Ludwig Haus, Darmstadt, 1901.
Main entrance doorway

24

be seen in their work after 1918; it was a change consistent not only with a new situation but also with a new point of view. Poelzig, the prewar Individualist for example, is very different from Poelzig the postwar Expressionist, as a comparison between his buildings for part of the 1913 Breslau Centenary Exhibition and the interior of the Berlin *Grosses Schauspielhaus* (1919) designed some six years later shows.

In the postwar phase in Berlin, the work of the older generation and the younger men overlaps, involving not only Poelzig, Behrens and Taut but also Erich Mendelsohn, the Luckhardt brothers, Max Taut, Hugo Häring, Walter Gropius, Mies van der Rohe and Hans Scharoun. Outside Berlin, Fritz Höger, Paul Bonatz, Bernhard Hoetger and Hermann Finsterlin were also caught up in the Expressionistic atmosphere. It is a fact of some importance that a number of these architects were products of the same school, the *Hochschule* at Charlottenburg. Outside Germany, other architects were also involved in work, although of a less extreme nature than the paper schemes of the German architects, that suggested close ties to Expressionism: the buildings designed by the so-called Amsterdam school, which came to light through the pages of the magazine *Wendingen* and the unique contribution made by Rudolf Steiner.

From these individuals and groups came the few finished buildings and the many unrealized (and in many cases unrealizable) paper projects that are characteristic of the Expressionist interlude: Poelzig's *Grosses Schauspielhaus*, Berlin 1919, and the Salzburg *Festspielhaus* competition projects, 1920–3; the Einstein Tower at Potsdam by Mendelsohn, which was projected as early as 1917 and erected between 1919–21; Fritz Höger's *Chilehaus* at Hamburg, 1923; the extensive schemes for apartment houses situated mainly in the suburbs of Amsterdam by de Klerk, Kramer and other Dutch architects after 1913, and the Goetheanum buildings at Dornach, near Basel in Switzerland by Rudolf Steiner, again dating from 1913 onwards. All of these buildings as well as the activities of the many Utopian groups formed in Berlin during the period immediately following the Armistice will be described in detail in later chapters. Somewhat paradoxically, it was from outside Germany that the term 'Expressionist' appears to have been used first to describe the work of practising architects. H. Th. Wijdeveld the architect-editor of the Dutch magazine *Wendingen* used the epithet in an article in the magazine in 1919 to describe the work of Kramer, La Croix, Staal, Blaauw and Kropholler in the Park Meerwijk, Bergen. The term was used again in *Wendingen* in 1920 by the German critic Oskar Beyer in an article on Erich Mendelsohn's Berlin exhibition entitled 'Architectuur in Ijzer en Beton'. Henry Russell-Hitchcock, certainly the most perceptive of the early international critics of modern architecture used the term very loosely in his book *Modern Architecture: Romanticism and Reintegration*, which was published in New York in 1929, when he referred to the influence of the Expressionist painters on the work of architects like Walter Gropius and his 'Expressionistic' Weimar Monument of 1920.

Of course, architecture is an expressive art form and whether this leads to stylistic, structural, symbolic or monumental expression is a matter of choice and intention on the part of the designer himself. Certainly the differences between the work of the Dutch and German architects of the time were emphasized by this very choice and intention as well as by the interests of national aspirations. There were similarities in Dutch and German Expressionist architecture, both in the use of materials and in the employment of free plan shapes. But they were very different, both in their approach to the expressive nature of architectural form and in the detailed handling of masses. For example, Dutch architects seemed to produce designs that looked particularly old-fashioned and picturesque; they emphasized the use of brick to give large areas of curved brickwork and revived the traditional handicraft techniques of stone and brick carving, and only occasionally made any real attempt to create a new spatial architecture. Such an attempt can be seen in the scheme designed for the *Eigen Haard* Housing Association along the Zaanstraat, Amsterdam, by Michel de Klerk in 1917. The German architects on the contrary were more conscious of the new-found liberty of three-dimensional form and often emphasized either the vertical or the horizontal elements, sometimes to a markedly exaggerated degree, in their designs. For them a building was itself a significant object with its purpose expressed in its simple functional layout and order as well as in its outward forms. To the German mind too, each building was something of a monument; a monument to national taste and pride. This aspect can be seen in the prewar monumental industrial buildings of Behrens and Poelzig and in such buildings as the Railway Station at Stuttgart (1911–27) designed by Paul Bonatz and E. F. Scholar.

In Germany during the postwar period of intense and seemingly irrational experiments with architectural ideas on paper, it was clear that society had to be completely reconstructed. The architecture that is now called Expressionist with its free, plastic, unconventional nature lent itself to such concepts and presented architects with the forms of a Utopia. The terms used by Bruno Taut and the other Utopian planners in the Berlin circle to describe their work—visionary, fantastic, dream, formplay—are the expressive essence of the time (a '*reine Utopie*') and the motivating forces behind even the political hopes of the nation. The words of Taut's original Proclamation of the role of the new architecture were echoed time and again:

'Art is quite a thing when it is art. Today it is not so. The severed lines of development can only be unified under the auspices of a new architecture so that each individual discipline will contribute to it. Then there will be no barrier between the crafts, sculpture and painting, it will all be one: architecture. Building is the immediate bearer of spiritual powers, shaping the feelings of the community, who slumber today and awake tomorrow. Both must be deliberate—the architects of today must plan the development of building. The community must enable and support their work for the future.'[2]

Visionary architecture, to Taut at least, was a challenge to 'build the world nearer to the heart's desire'. Unlike the related movements in painting, *Die Brücke* and *Der Blaue Reiter*, both of which had a self-determined role to play, architecture during its visionary phase remained free to explore its own romantic laws and principles. It was an exploration that was to take Bruno Taut to the height of Alpine peaks with his Scheerbartian version of a world of coloured concrete and glass and Hans Poelzig back to the rococo with his projects for the Salzburg *Festspielhaus*.

Historically there has always been a place in architectural speculation for concepts of this kind. Fantasy and *Phantastische Architektur* goes back to the 'Antichi Edifici' of Giovanni Battista Piranesi in the eighteenth century, and to the imaginative designs of the French Symbolist Claude-Nicholas Ledoux (1736–1806). Its revival is apparent in the work of the National Romantic architects during the last years of the nineteenth century as well as in the *Art Nouveau*, and probably most importantly today—for again there is a similar 'visionary' interest in some circles—in the peculiarly eccentric buildings of Antonio Gaudí in Barcelona. Gaudí's work more than anyone else's outside the German speaking *Jugendstil* circle seems even as early as the turn of the century to 'possess in embryo the body of Expressionist' architecture, with its free curving façades, a general solidity of form, inventive and weighty structure, and its concern for the monumental aspects and symbolic qualities of building. The elements of religious symbolism as well as of fantasy found in Gaudí's work come close to those found in the work of later Expressionists.

In Rudolf Wiene's Expressionist film *The Cabinet of Dr Caligari* (1920) the outdoor sets constructed by Hermann Warm and his team of designers reflect in the use of twisted pathways and walls the eccentricities of the walls and landscaping in Gaudí's designs for the Parc Güell in Barcelona. Although Gaudí's style was a distinctly personal one, which had little to do with fashionable international art trends of the time, its 'frenzy', as Pevsner calls it, bridges the historicism of the late nineteenth century to 1920. Gaudí's obsession with the idea of a spiritualized geometry (e.g. he likened the geometrical surfaces of the hyperbolic paraboloid to the Holy Trinity) were paralleled to some extent in the theory Rudolf Steiner propounded on the symbolic and spiritual significance of form in his Dornach lectures. It was something he also attempted to formulate in his concept of 'spiritual' building. Indeed, as George Collins has written, Steiner was: 'weaving Goethe's ideas on nature into a theory of directly expressive architecture that has much in common with the effect of Gaudí's actual buildings'.[3]

It was suggested earlier that the outbreak of the war in 1914 had left the ideas for a new architecture in embryo, but not before it had been firmly established that the architecture of this time was to be, like its predecessor, the *Art Nouveau*, distinctly anti-traditional. This anti-traditional attitude was even true of Holland—the most tradition-bound of all the countries engaged in the pioneer period of modern architecture—and reflected in the first important building of the 'Amsterdam School', the *Scheepvaarthuis*, by J. M. van der Meij, de Klerk and Kramer in 1912–13.

The industrial and economic expansion that had taken place in Germany before 1914 had presented a handful of men with a vision of a new architecture that was coming to terms with the advances in technology and industry. Much of the groundwork for this approach had been done by Hermann Muthesius, who had been instrumental in founding the *Deutscher Werkbund* in 1907, and who had, three years earlier in 1904, presented to the German public his assessment of the English domestic architectural scene—largely in terms of the Arts and Crafts movement—in his three-volume work *Das Englische Haus*. It was the *Werkbund* Exhibition of 1914 at Cologne that brought the ideas for a new architecture to a head. Politically, practically and theoretically the Exhibition provided German architects with a summary of the way the future would lie. It was the real public birthplace of dynamic

27

architecture. The three buildings of importance at the Exhibition: van de Velde's Model Theatre; Gropius and Meyer's office and factory building; and Bruno Taut's pavilion for the German glass industry, combined a mixture of the romantic, the objective and the exploratory. These three very dissimilar structures, while stressing prewar Expressionist leanings, also suggested the *Neue Sachlichkeit* and in so doing demonstrated the power and direction of the *Werkbund* itself.

Van de Velde's Theatre, a product of the mind that had played father to the *Art Nouveau*, was without doubt the most convincing building he ever designed, with its classically organized plan a contrast to the moulded forms of the exterior, which stress the plasticity of the building. With this building van de Velde had disassociated himself completely from the *Jugendstil* type of decoration that was very common in entertainment buildings just before the war, and found a truly architectural solution in the building's solidity and sculptural form.

Taut's small Glass Pavilion had totally different qualities, the inner volumes are not governed by the effects of the external forms as in van de Velde's Theatre; with the pavilion the architect was wrestling with the Scheerbartian idea of extending the interior of his building outwards, by means of glass, colour and light.

The Office Building and Hall of Machinery by Walter Gropius at the Exhibition was symmetrically planned like both van de Velde's Theatre and Taut's Pavilion. It was not a building complex as frankly new as the Fagus Factory he had designed with Adolf Meyer at Alfeld some three years earlier, but it indicated in its clear planning and in the elevational simplicity of the office façade—even with its debt to

*Plan of the Werkbund Exhibition, Cologne, 1914*

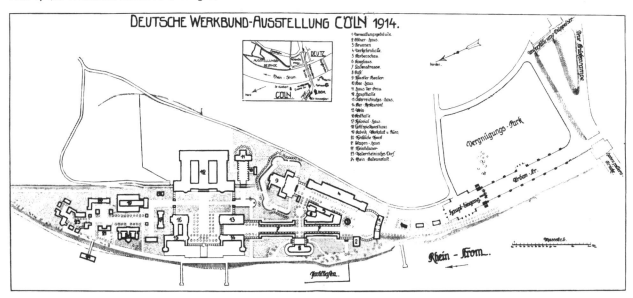

Model Theatre at the
Werkbund Exhibition,
Cologne, 1914. Architect:
Henri van de Velde. Ground
floor plan and front
elevation

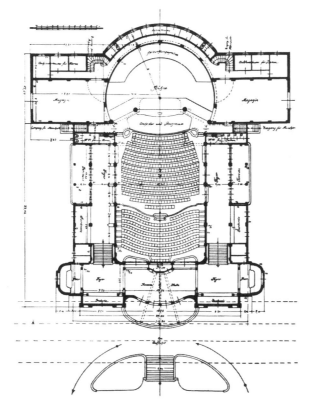

29

*Bruno Taut: staircase of the Glass Pavilion, Cologne, 1914*

Frank Lloyd Wright's Mason City Bank Building in Iowa—a clear premonition of the aesthetic discipline of Functionalism. The introduction of the glazed staircase motif was wilful romanticism, as clearly Scheebartian as Taut's bubble.

These three buildings demonstrated three ways of approaching the problem of architecture: the plastic form way of Van de Velde; the visionary way of Taut; and the mechanistic, technological way of Gropius. All three designers in this exhibition had made a firm stand against any kind of eclecticism and all three showed a concern for the expressive content of architectural form. When once again after the war years architects were able to pick up their pencils to redraw a plan for a new society, it was with these three buildings at the back of their minds. It was to be a 'golden' period.

*Model Factory by Walter Gropius at the Exhibition, Cologne, 1914*

# 4

# Peter Behrens and the Individualists

Undoubtedly the most important figure in prewar German architecture was Peter Behrens (1868–1940), although the originality of his work is at times more than matched by his contemporary Hans Poelzig (1869–1936).[1]

Other architects who presented radically new ideas at that time include the City architect of Breslau, Max Berg (1870–1948) and the group that came under his and Poelzig's influence in that city; the younger architect Bruno Taut (1880–1938), who worked with his brother Max Taut and Franz Hoffmann mainly from Berlin, and who had strong connections with such early Expressionist writers as Paul Scheerbart; Walter Gropius and Adolf Meyer who were responsible for what has been called the 'first building of the modern movement', the Fagus Factory at Alfeld a.d. Leine (1911–13), as well as such isolated figures as Heinrich Tessenow, who designed the layout and many of the houses in the garden city of Hellerau, near Dresden, and Alfred Grenander who was responsible for the *Hochbahn* and *Untergrundbahn* in Berlin.

Only a year separated Behrens and Poelzig in age. Both had come to architecture from different directions; Behrens from the *Jugendstil* circle in Munich where he had been active as a painter, graphic artist and designer and Poelzig from the Technical High School in Charlottenburg. Behrens and Poelzig both possessed a thorough knowledge of the practical side of building allied to an extremely personal attitude to architectural design and education. They were the Individualists who saw that the architect of the time had not only a responsibility to make a building the working answer to a number of practical and functional questions but also to make his creation something of a monument in its own right as well as a symbol of its time. They were responsible for the erection of a number of major industrial buildings built in Germany before the First World War and both received the active support of the founder of the *Werkbund*, Hermann Muthesius. Both became strong advocates of the *Werkbund* policy to establish close ties between industry and the designer.

In 1907 Behrens was made director of design to the great electrical combine the A.E.G., Berlin, and within a short while he was able to put some of his ideas for new industrial buildings and product design

Peter Behrens: a study for a summer villa, 1904

Peter Behrens: own house, Darmstadt, 1901

into practice. The massive Turbine Erecting Shop built on the Huttenstrasse in Berlin in 1909 was his first major achievement. By bringing in the professional services of a man like Behrens to take responsibility in matters of design A.E.G. were setting an historical precedent. The Kaiser's demand for the wedding of progressive industry to politics and art was taking place.

Six or so years before he joined A.E.G. Behrens began to dissociate himself from the curvilinear and ornamental *Jugendstil*, the style he had adequately mastered in Munich, preferring to create an architecture more geometrical and free from the excesses that this style demanded. His later buildings owed more to the Neo-Classicism of Schinkel than to the angular and emphatic stylistic motifs from which his own house—his first building—had stemmed on the Matildenhöhe at Darmstadt in 1901.

This first building was produced as part of the artistic colony on the Matildenhöhe that had been commissioned by Ernst Ludwig, Grand Duke of Hessen, from the group of artists, *Die Sieben*, that had been invited to Darmstadt in 1889. In 1903 Behrens was appointed to the post of director of the *Kunstgewerbeschule* at Düsseldorf and he remained there until 1907. It was also in 1903 that Poelzig became director of the *Kunstgewerbeschule* in Breslau where he had been a lecturer since 1899. In 1911 the school became part of the Academy and, still with Poelzig as director (until 1916), it became an extremely important educational establishment for architecture and painting.

Behrens's influence as a teacher spread beyond the existing educational establishments and eventually into his own Berlin office where he employed as pupil-assistants Walter Gropius (1907–10), Mies van der Rohe (1908–11) and Le Corbusier (1910–11). His influence as an architect spread throughout Europe. He designed the well-known house, 'New Ways', at Northampton for Bassett-Lowke in 1923, numerous projects for clients in Austria, and a number of pavilions for important international exhibitions. His architecture up to the war years was consistently frank in design, large scaled and yet distinctly orthodox. Only after the war did he attempt to produce buildings of a more romantic kind. Then Behrens, like so many of his contemporaries, was soon caught up in the Expressionist mood that had been created by painters, writers and sculptors and interpreted in architectural terms by a number of younger architects. No doubt by applying his famous *Werkbund* motto 'fitness for purpose' the little brick patterned Dombauhütte at the 1922 Munich Exhibition could be justified. This building, almost Dutch in its brickwork treatment like so much of the exhibition architecture at that time, was compelling and original, controlled both by practicability and a desire for novel expression.

In the building for the *I. G. Farbenindustrie Aktiengessellschaft* at Frankfurt-Höchst (1920–4)—a gigantic structure consisting of laboratories, workshops and offices—Behrens made a complete departure from the industrial prototypes he had produced earlier for the A.E.G. This building was a tremendous, anti-Classical structure which in its use of decorated brickwork bears a strong resemblance to the contemporary work of the Hamburg Expressionist Fritz Höger; the flamboyant entrance hall decoration too, with its corbelled bands of brickwork, is very near to the work of the Amsterdam school. The entrance hall rises like Frank Lloyd Wright's Larkin Building interior, through various floors of offices, and is glazed over by a shaped roof light, while the angular shapes of the brick piers—a common Expressionist motif—contrast with the strongly patterned floor tiles.

In such earlier buildings as the Water Tower and Gas Holders for the Frankfurt Gas Company of 1911–12 Behrens had shown that he was not completely held down by his Neo-Classical approach and there an example of a freer and more inventive use of form was made as a contrast to the rigidity of the façade treatment of the surrounding office and works buildings.[2]

In 1922 Behrens was appointed director of the Vienna Academy School of Architecture. Many of his own projects in the years that followed this appointment were as markedly Expressionist as those of his students, and have a touch and diversity about them that look as if he was trying desperately to keep in the swim. The study made for a Hotel at Brno of 1926 is clearly derived in part from Fritz Höger's Chile House in Hamburg (1923), while the *Architekturskizze zum Durchbruchsprojekt*, Berlin-Jägerstrasse 1927, looks as if it was directly inspired by the work of Hans Scharoun or the Luckhardt brothers.[3] Certainly, at this stage, when Behrens was sketching out ideas on paper, and when he was designing for exhibitions, he got to the roots of the Expressionist approach.

*AEG Turbine Erecting Shop, Berlin, 1909*

Gas Works and Waterworks buildings,
Frankfurt-am-Main, 1911

Hotel Project, Brno, 1926

There is a world of difference between the classically organized *Werkbund* building for Bern in 1917 and the chapel designed five years later for the Munich Exhibition, or even the Pavilion designed in 1925 for the Decorative Arts Exhibition in Paris. These latter buildings are gay—one might almost say tongue-in-cheek buildings—firmly establishing the temporary, slightly frivolous and symbolic nature of exhibition architecture, the kind of architecture in which the younger Expressionists excelled immediately after the war.

# 5

# Hans Poelzig and *Formenrausch*

Hans Poelzig was the most uncompromising and individualistic architect practising in Germany before the First World War; immediately after the war he assumed the role of progenitor-in-chief of the visionary phase of the Berlin circle. His influence as a teacher was equally strong. Inventiveness was the keynote of his early projects and after 1916 when he left the Academy of Arts at Breslau he developed a mood of fantasy with strange and extremely unorthodox designs often on a vast scale. Poelzig was born in Berlin the son of an Englishman, G. A. Ames, and the Countess Clara Henrietta Poelzig. The couple were divorced in 1870 and the child was given the aristocratic maiden name.

From 1888 to 1893 Hans Poelzig studied architecture at the Technical High School, in Berlin. Later, in 1899, he moved to Breslau, having taken up an appointment as lecturer in *Stilkunde* at the then *Kunstgewerbeschule*; from 1903 to 1916 he served as its director and saw the school's amalgamation with the Breslau Academy in 1911. From 1916 to 1920 he was the city architect to Dresden as well as professor at the City's Technical High School. In 1920 he returned to Berlin.

In each of his early prewar projects Poelzig showed a diversity of approach to the problem of handling architectural form, and a desire to express simply and clearly the purpose of the building. Examples of his work from the prewar era that show his inventiveness to the best advantage include the Water Mill project of 1908; the Water Tower and Exhibition Hall built in 1910–11; the Chemical Factory at Luban, near Posen, of 1911–12, and the Office Building at Breslau in 1911–12.

'Architecture', Poelzig said, in his address on the occasion of the revival of the *Deutscher Werkbund* in 1919, 'is the product of a national state of mind', which, he claimed, can only be achieved as an *ars magna* '. . . where the conviction has been established that we have to create for eternity.'[1]

This attitude is reflected in most of Poelzig's work, in his attempt to imbue each building with a sense of Germanic monumentality, and with the quality of durability. Paradoxically, the building he designed in 1914 as an actual monument, the Bismarck Memorial, high on the banks of the Rhine above Bingen, was one of his least successful works. Looking as if it were constructed from the vertebrae of some gigantic prehistoric animal, it possesses none of the inventiveness seen in the earlier industrial projects, such as the monumentally shaped Water Tower he designed for the Posen Exhibition of 1911. This tower was a remarkable example of Poelzig's attempt to marry 'purpose' to 'fantasy'.

Like Behrens's Turbine Shop for the A.E.G. on the Huttenstrasse in Berlin, but eschewing that building's mild classicism, the Water Tower overcame the conventional ugliness usually associated with industrial buildings. Externally it was a great heptagonal steel-framed structure, with panels of brick and glass fitting flush with the vertical framing. The ground floor, which was the widest part of the structure, was to serve as a market-hall, after being used initially as an exhibition hall. A strange enough building from the outside, the interior was a mechanical labyrinth of lattice girders and steep spiral staircases. In a drawing of the vast interior of the lower part of the tower, Poelzig shows people in evening dress walking among the enormous lattice girders as if it were the set for some esoteric Expressionist drama. Two years after the completion of the Posen Water Tower the Centenary Hall at Breslau, designed by Max Berg and the engineer Trauer, was opened. This building, like the Water Tower, employed the use of new constructional techniques.

At Breslau reinforced concrete was used to construct the vast auditorium, consisting of a large centrally domed area with smaller apsidal spaces. It was one of the first of such building types to be designed by a practising architect. It still exists today as a People's Hall. Indeed, apart from its sheer structural inventiveness, it is one of the largest domed spaces that has ever been constructed, having an internal diameter of just over 200 feet. The concrete ribs of the large dome fan out from the central ring beam to rest on vast arched supports, themselves supported by secondary ribs. The glazing runs around the interior of the dome in concentric bands as clerestory windows stepped back from the main structural shape.

*Study for a water mill, Breslau, 1908*

*Chemical Factory, Luban, 1911–12. The main building*

The Hall of History that Poelzig designed for the same exhibition at Breslau in 1913 seems a puny attempt to recreate a Neo-Classical atmosphere when it is compared to Berg's building, and its concern with what Poelzig termed 'formulating a new and liberated Greek Doric order . . .' suggests a retrograde step.

Eclectisism, both from medieval and Classical sources, still played an important part in the architecture of Poelzig and his generation. Behrens's work too is saturated in the Neo-Classicism of the *Schinkelschule*, as his German Embassy Building for Leningrad shows. Even as late as 1922 Adolf Loos, the Viennese champion of plain, unadorned surfaces, submitted an entry for the *Chicago Tribune* Tower Competition in the form of a single multi-storey Doric order as if by itself the order had an eternal monumental quality.

The monumental aspect of Poelzig's work can also be detected in the remarkably efficient, although very diverse, buildings he designed to house the plant of the Luban Chemical Works near Posen, Silesia, in 1911–12. Here the quest for the monumental was more subtle. Buildings of various shapes and sizes were coordinated to give a sense of unity to the whole project. Brick walls were punched with window openings, some square, others semicircular, and these ran in parallel bands around the various parts of the factory façades expressing its simple load-bearing structure.

The roofs, which in some cases were stepped like those of Tyrolean chalets, were almost flat and provided another unifying factor—a horizontal emphasis. But it was the use of the semicircular window that was so surprising and unusual, although it had been introduced as a decorative device in the much earlier unbuilt project for a Water Mill in 1908. In this first study Poelzig had scattered semicircular window openings, haphazardly it seems, over the curved brickwork ends of his two buildings, and contrasted them with large areas of steel-framed glazing units on the facing façades between the two parallel blocks. The blocks were joined by the glazed bridge spanning between the areas of this 'curtain walling', and over the lock. In both these projects Poelzig successfully married his own personal feeling for the plasticity of form to an expression of pierced brickwork that bears strong resemblance to engineer-designed nineteenth-century warehouse structures.

By reducing architecture to its simplest terms Poelzig also produced a striking idea for an office building in Breslau in 1912. This building, though heavy and lacking finesse in its detailing, introduced the horizontal band window alternating with a continuous masonry cornice at each storey height; the five-storey structure itself curving freely around its corner site. Some years later these very motifs—the curved façade and the horizontal bands of window—were to be greatly refined and re-used by architects such as Erich Mendelsohn, the Luckhardts and Mies van der Rohe in their store and office projects. These features soon became the hallmark of modern commercial architecture.

During the war years the *Werkbund* organized a competition for a House of Friendship to be built in Istanbul.[2] It was to be erected to help establish a closer link between the German and Turkish nations, who were then allies. Poelzig's answer to the problem was a vast terraced building shaped like a giant flight of steps, which internally was to be divided into numerous courts and hanging gardens. By sheer size it was to dominate the old city, commanding an uninterrupted view of the Bosphorus. Poelzig attempted, with his Friendship House in 1917, to free his architecture of all European precedents, thus creating his own personal kind of *Formenrausch* that was to find even greater freedom in his later postwar projects. The series of arched panels and vertical divisions that are seen in the House of Friendship were introduced again in the most famous of Poelzig's buildings, the *Grosses Schauspielhaus*

*Poelzig's competition entry for the House of Friendship, Istanbul, 1917*

42

*Office building in Breslau, Junkernstrasse, 1911–12*

*Chemical Factory, Luban. Storage buildings*

Water Tower and Exhibition building, Posen,
1911. Main entrance

Right: Interior of the Water Tower at
restaurant level

Left: Chemical Factory, Luban. The decorative
treatment of the windows presents a contrast
to the vast area of plain brickwork of the gable
wall

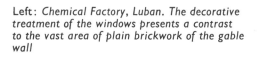

Left: *Interior of the Water Tower showing the exhibition space*

Right: *Max Berg: Centenary Hall, Breslau, 1912–13. The sober exterior*

*Interior of the Centenary Hall*

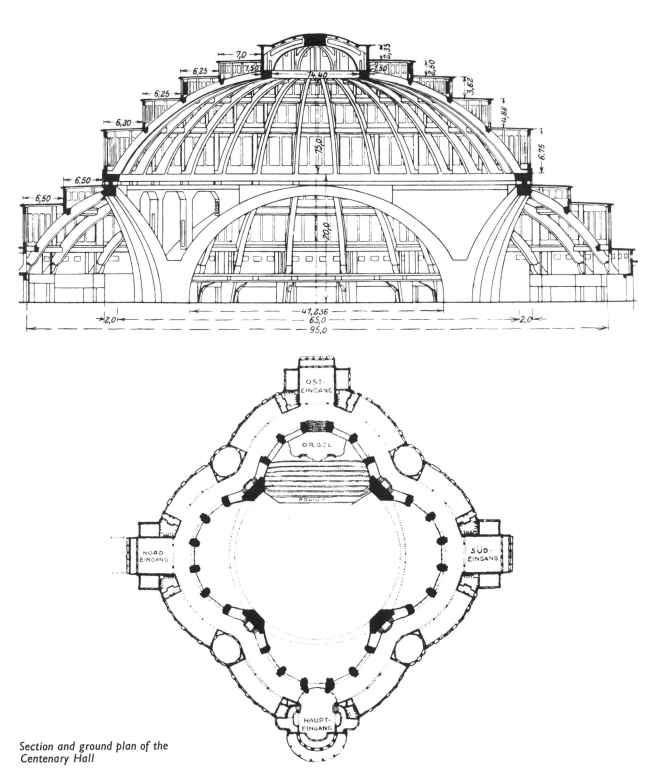

*Section and ground plan of the Centenary Hall*

The Centenary Hall. A view of one of the apsidal arches

The inside of the Centenary Hall showing the gigantic reinforced concrete structure supporting the balcony within one of the four apses

*Drawing showing the layout of the Centennial buildings, Breslau*

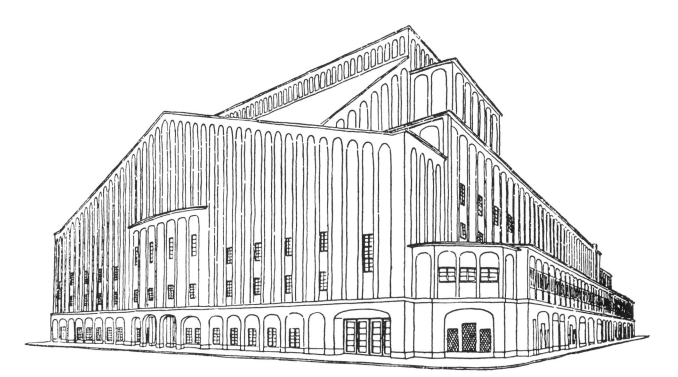

*Hans Poelzig*: Grosses Schauspielhaus, *Berlin, 1919*

*Entrance of* the Grosses Schauspielhaus

Above and right: *The interior of the* Grosses Schauspielhaus, *showing the hanging icicle forms around the dome, and the concealed lighting effect*

in Berlin, which he designed in collaboration with, and for, Max Reinhardt, the brilliant director of the *Deutsches Theater*, in 1919.

A man of equal talent, Reinhardt had revolutionized stage production in Germany before the war by substituting the stage architect for the scene painter and by eliminating the barrier of the stage between the actor and the audience in his *Tribune* theatre. As H. F. Garten has said: 'For him the stage was not merely a faithful mirror of reality but a magic world radiating its own light'.[3]

In the case of the *Grosses Schauspielhaus* Poelzig created, out of the old rambling market-hall which had also housed the famous *Zirkus Schumann*, a fantasy in which Reinhardt's magic world came to life. It seated an audience of five thousand and had a stage area big enough to play dramas that demanded enough space for great crowd scenes. The stage projected right into the body of the hall, while the

building envelope itself was like some giant inverted Expressionist stage set, with a cavernous interior festooned with tier upon tier of hanging icicle forms that ran round the old gallery levels.

In his article on Poelzig in the *Architectural Review* in 1923, Hermann Scheffauer calls the building 'one of Poelzig's greatest triumphs' and gives a striking description of the forcefulness of its design: 'Elaborating and illuminating his practical problem in the light of his fantasy, Poelzig saw his architectural-theatrical mission thus; first, to prepare the spectator for something extraordinary, something that would seduce him from reality—through the mere externals of the building. This end he achieved by the striking way in which he forced the interior to impose its will upon the exterior, by the monumental way in which the great masses ascend, climb over and intersect one another—a severe and grandiose up-piling of bulk upon bulk, like the *massif* of a mountain. The form was accentuated by the colour, a deep and vibrant port-wine red in which the immense arched façades are dyed. From the naked, red-tinted crypts and corridors, the theatre devotee was brought into the vast and brilliant auditorium with its enormous dome of pendent stalactite forms poised magically overhead and studded with myriads of light-points, the great voids and terraces of the stage, and the tiers of seats.'

Indeed, as Scheffauer goes on to say: 'The sculpturesque is so strong a feature of Poelzig's genius that there remains about most of his creations the impression of having been cast in one molten throw, or hewn with boldest strokes with a modelling tool out of some plastic material.'[4] If any building deserved the epithet Expressionist it was certainly this work of Poelzig's imagination, in which the free forms of the interior are closely woven into a clearly practical design. In Poelzig's concept the 'imagination is not fettered by practicability and the sense of purpose; it is from these very things it derives the power to become creative'.[5]

Due to the eclectic mannerisms indicated in this theatre and the startling appearance of its interior, the dramatic exhibitionist quality of its architecture caused considerable controversy and comment. Mendelsohn compared its plain façade to *St Maria della Grazie* in Milan and wrote in glowing terms of the fantastic spatial effects of its interior 'where . . . the circular foyer is very beautiful and everywhere big in its details'. It was described as 'a child of the war and of the Revolution of the Empire and the Republic' in a contemporary magazine.

On the occasion of the revival of the *Werkbund* in 1919 Poelzig restated his views and his hopes for a strong vigorous new handicraft and architectural tradition in his vice-presidential address. This document provides a valuable insight into the aims of the Werkbund itself as well as into the thought of the most respected of the older Individualist architects. After a discussion on the foundation of the *Werkbund* as a spiritual movement, with its tenets based on the marriage of handicrafts and art, Poelzig restates the case that the *Werkbund* 'does not want to be merely a mediator or instigator of industrial art'. For here he saw a danger in machine forms being adapted for design ends, particularly in building: 'It is necessary', he said, 'that the artistic element is present which makes use of technical possibilities, but which is in itself able to shape the form of the building.'

Drawing analogies between engineering and architectural projects, he went on:

'The average engineer will build a bad water tower or a bad factory as far as the form is concerned; the average architect who thinks he is only doing his duty by working from the outside, offers an even worse water tower or factory. All relatively perishable things which have to be superseded by better technical achievements when the time comes, can only be designed by the engineer, but all those buildings which are to remain for even 30–50 years as buildings must have form, which originates from the architectonic creative urge of the artist, with strict observance of the technical principles. Our "building skill" has, as far as techniques is concerned, better and richer possibilities than in the Middle Ages; it is however, just as well possible to give the concrete or steel construction of a wooden warehouse a form which is in agreement with the essence of its construction. That compromises only deteriorate and lead to impurity of style is evident in the technical buildings in which one tried to follow the old and accepted rhythmic laws, as for example of Antiquity, or which try to hide themselves behind an architectonic masque which in point of fact is in contradiction with the logical coherence of the applied construction.'[6]

Poelzig goes on to make a further analysis of the problem of style in modern terms:

'The coming time of poverty seems to me an opportunity to divest architecture of impurities of style. The means are few and compel us to limitations. Let us not follow Schinkel who stressed the adoption of perfect antique forms and discipline, nor a mixture of different rhythmic principles which are meant to be considered as richness of imagination, but which are nothing but cheap fancy. Architecture is the product of a national state of mind and the average deplorable architecture of German towns during the last few years was a result of the corruption of a nation, which desired only material gain, a nation which had lost the psychic connection with its native soil. . . . Our aim is to reconnect them again. We can only do this by means of a change of attitude, by the resuscitation of satisfaction of labour.'[7]

After discussing the situation and training of architects in Germany he makes the final plea that the *Werkbund* should again attempt to bring handicraft techniques and art together to prevent a rise 'of an art or handicraft proletariat'.

With little or no building work being carried out in Germany just after the war it was not surprising, with Poelzig's reputation, that an invitation should come from Austria for the design for a new *Festspielhaus* for the historic city of Salzburg. The idea for a festival at Salzburg came initially from Hugo von Hofmannsthal who founded with Max Reinhardt a committee to consider the possibilities of erecting a permanent musical centre. In the summer of 1919 Alfred Roller sent out invitations to Josef Hoffmann, the renowned Viennese Sezession architect, and to Hans Poelzig to produce designs in competition for the projected Festival Hall.

Nothing, however, emerged from Hoffmann's drawing-board; had it done so it would certainly have been very different from the frankly Expressionist design submitted by Poelzig in 1920.[8] This project was to become Poelzig's most ambitious *oeuvre* and although it was destined not to be realized in the flesh, a number of alternative schemes were submitted by the architect to the committee. The Baroque Park just outside the city of Salzburg was selected as the site for this immense project, and Poelzig in his first scheme took advantage of the hilly nature of the site to create, in Mozart's own town, a personal 'magic mountain' as a truly rococo image. The requirements of the committee included a large festival theatre seating two thousand people, a smaller *Mozart-Saal* to accommodate eight hundred people and many other ancillary rooms including workshops, studios and a restaurant. In the first scheme, a giant building like a brooding monster sat on the top of the slope, while Gothic-like arcades, designed to keep the approaching visitor dry, connected it to the entrances at the base of the site. The whole thing was designed as if the interior of the *Grosses Schauspielhaus* had been inverted, so that this time the exterior of this gangling building grew up like rows of stalagmites from a basically pyramidal structure, while the octopus-shaped plan spread itself around the site, clutching ancillary structures in its arms. A most fantastic folly indeed, which the Festival Committee were unable to accept because of lack of funds.

In 1921 Poelzig submitted a much smaller and simpler building to the committee. This time the riot of rising and writhing forms gave way to the use of crisp rectangular and circular shapes. A series of truncated cones, gradually diminishing in scale, were piled one upon the other and pierced by continuous bands of arched openings; the interior, a vast mysterious cavern, was lit by a single source of light at the centre. The use of bands of arched openings, mainly for loggias, was common to all the schemes, but only the last revised design brought them under any strict geometric control. But all these attempts to shape the building into a condition so that it would be acceptable economically failed, and

*Salzburg* Festspielhaus.
*Interior sketch, 1922*

*Hans Poelzig's design for the set of Der Golem*

*The 'Capitol', Berlin*

even though the final scheme had been reduced to a single structure it was never constructed.

Film was another medium in which Hans Poelzig was able to display his interest in fantasy and the plasticity of architectural form. In 1920 he designed the settings for the remake of Paul Wegener's UFA film, *Der Golem*, a fantasy based on a Jewish medieval legend about a clay figure that is brought to life and develops into a powerful robot. The scenery consisted of Gaudíesque mazes of crooked houses and irregular streets, making up a medieval ghetto.

Poelzig was also an accomplished painter and draughtsman. P. Morton Shand said of his sketches, in a review of Heuss's *Hans Poelzig: Bauten und Entwürfe*, in the *Architectural Review*, that 'Mendelsohn seems to have derived his soft-lead impressionist technique from them'.[9]

When building activity was resumed in Germany Poelzig continued to design buildings on a monumental scale, and after he became Professor of the Technical High School at Charlottenburg in 1923, an appointment he held until 1936, he was responsible for many large and complex structures. These included the 'Capitol' cinema of 1925 and the vast *Messegelände* of 1927, both in Berlin. But with these buildings he had clearly thrown off any leanings towards Expressionism and was more closely allied to the work being produced by Berlin architects generally, which had by that time become rigidly geometric.

# Vision, Fantasy and Utopia

**3**

# Postwar Expressionist architecture in Germany

Two streams of development ran through the architecture of the postwar German Expressionist phase. One stream emphasized the more traditional aspects of architecture and a traditional use of materials, and was represented by architects like Fritz Höger (best known for his *Chilehaus* at Hamburg, 1923), Wilhelm Kreis (who designed the Düsseldorf *Gesolei* buildings in 1926) and Bernhard Hoetger, the sculptor (who built among other things the eccentric Paula Modersohn-Becker Haus at Bremen, 1926–8). The other stream, a visionary one, owed more to an attempt to provide architecture with a new basis and can now be considered as an important part of the 'fabric' of the Modern Movement in architecture. In this second stream the buildings of Erich Mendelsohn during his Expressionist phase would be included together with the flamboyant and dynamic designs of the Luckhardt brothers; the theoretical ideas of Bruno Taut and the 'Glass Chain Group', 1919–23; the paper *Formspiel* architecture of Hermann Finsterlin as well as those few, very few, buildings, projects and monuments designed by Mies van der Rohe and Walter Gropius that were clearly displaying an absorption with, if not a conviction of, the Expressionist attitude. The traditional stream outlived the visionary phase by about ten years. Visionary or expressionistic architecture seemed to presume a certain irrational attitude to design, as well as a symbolistic, romantic approach; it was a Dionysian trait in a predominantly revolutionary *milieu*. It touched almost all the architects in practice in Berlin, as well as others working outside the city. It was essentially an architecture from Utopia.

Though an antirational tendency, the architecture of this immediate postwar period must not be considered as the negation of the later and dissimilar *Neue Sachlichkeit* approach. This it certainly was not. The postwar interlude of Expressionism was rather a phase on the way to the 'New Architecture'— a short visionary, experimental and fantastic episode deep in the heart of Modern Movement developments, that lasted in Berlin a little over four years from 1918 to 1923. In whatever way it appears to our own generation, with all its immaturity and often wildly crude forms, it must be given its rightful place in the mainstream of development. Indeed, some of the ideas the architecture of the visionary phase possessed and promoted have been found useful today, even though it became impossible to assimilate them into the straight line mechanistic aesthetic of Modern Movement's 'International Functionalist' phase during the late twenties.

Expressionist architecture was mainly confined to paper, and there were few built examples. Work that was carried out, such as Poelzig's remodelling of the old *Zirkus Schumann* in Berlin as the *Schauspielhaus* and Mendelsohn's Einstein Tower at Potsdam, underlined the impact of a new sensibility that had begun to show itself late in 1918.

Thus we can now speak of the *Zeitgeist*, the spirit of an age that transcends the verbal, visual and pictorial illusions invented by the writers, architects and artists of an era; an aura of society that finds at least a basis in the formulations and concepts of thinkers and philosophers alike. The existentialist thought of the previous century had aggravated the air for the personal, emotional attitude of Expressionism and this was reflected in the architecture of this postwar era, in its deformation, its passion and its sensitivity. The architecture of this period was one of protest. It was this form of protest —itself a new element—that, as Gregotti says:

'. . . moves naturally from nihilism to a ''mystic return to one's origins'', rather than opposition; this protest existed autonomously with respect to the real conditions of society, and offered no alternatives; so that its most energetic artistic results were achieved in satire, in deformation, which emphasized the arbitrary character of the expressive form, and in the use of the caricature, which is of course the image of the grotesque discrepancy between reality and appearance.'

Gregotti goes on to say:

'It should be noted that though this character of ''deformation'' was one of the most authentic elements of expressionism, it was somehow transmitted to the successive ''*Neue Sachlichkeit*'' (witness the music of Hindemith or Weill, and the architecture of rationalism) and through this somehow summed up a few nationalist elements, taking on a meaning which, despite its international tone, it was not to have in other countries.'[1]

In Germany the armistice of 11 November 1918 had brought the struggle in Europe to a close. Almost immediately Berlin became the centre of renewed architectural activity and speculation, gradually assuming its role as the second artistic capital in Europe, after Paris. In the politically confused city, the young progressive architects and artists, many of whom had spent long periods fighting at the front, quickly joined or formed groups for discussion and propaganda purposes.

Although it was a period of intense creative activity for most of the architects in Berlin there was a general lack of direction in all the projects. There was no single stylistic issue common to any of the groups, hardly in fact a single common idea. Enthusiasm abounded. The individualism that had been latent in the prewar architecture was made manifest in the postwar period. However, as Bruno Taut wrote much later in his book *Modern Architecture*, it was not just a case of picking up the strands left from the prewar era and carrying on from there: 'It was not possible to make use of any pre-War traditions, for that period was perforce regarded as the cause of the misfortunes of the past, and because every achievement of those days seemed more or less to hang together with the origins of war.'[2]

Ideals were at stake in the postwar era; ideals that would be established in terms of a happy future and a vital new art movement. The challenge of the time in architecture and the arts was as much emotional and political as it was creative. Talk of revolution was everywhere in the air. The struggling Social-Democratic government was weak, disorganized and completely incapable of dealing with the sustained inflation. The efforts to restore order were further aggravated by the assassination of the leaders of the *Spartacus* communist cell, Rosa Luxemburg and Karl Liebknecht on 15 January 1919. Politically, socially and spiritually the Expressionist warning previously heralding the storm of war had taken on a new meaning. It was time for a reappraisal of man in society, a chance for the establishment of the Nietzscheian type of new man, the super artist. The artists in Germany and particularly in the Berlin of 1918 found their most immediate outlet in the formation of the *Novembergruppe*, a 'union of radical creative artists', which as its title implies, was founded during the Armistice month. The group was predominantly left-wing and represented largely the radical prewar Expressionism propagated by anarchist periodicals such as Franz Pfemfert's *Die Aktion*, and *Revolution*. Its membership was drawn from all disciplines and eventually included architects, painters, musicians, film producers, critics and art historians. The Group quickly became the focal point of creative thinking and activity in Berlin. Within the *Novembergruppe* architecture was given pride of place and re-established as a social art; without reconstruction on a grand and creative scale, it was felt, none of the arts could flourish. To this end, in real revolutionary language, the group published an inaugural circular that demanded interest and collaboration in architectural projects together with pleas for the reorganization of art teaching and legislation for the arts.

The distinguished members of the *Novembergruppe* brought a new serious tone to the discussion of the place of the arts in the bewildered Germany, and it attracted to its forums not only men of high intellectual and creative ability but also men who were prepared to support financially and to propagate actively the new ideas of experimenters such as Berthold Brecht, Erich Mendelsohn, Viking Eggeling, Paul Hindemith and Alban Berg. The most successful propaganda vehicle for the group was the exhibition and many of these were held in private galleries and public places throughout Berlin during 1919–20. On 18 November 1918 the initial formation of the *Arbeitsrat für Kunst* took place in Berlin. This 'Workers' Council for Art', with its aims of liberating 'art from decades of tutelage' and 'unifying art and the people', was in effect a working and study organization and therefore somewhat different from the propagandist *Novembergruppe*. The *Novembergruppe* had a large membership scattered throughout Germany while the *Arbeitsrat*, whose title implied left-wing sympathies (the German word *Arbeiterrat* means 'Soviet'), had a selective membership and was centred on Berlin. The *Arbeitsrat* became more closely tied, as a working division, to the *Novembergruppe* after November 1919, and was finally dissolved as a separate official body on 30 May 1921.[3]

Within the *Arbeitsrat für Kunst*, under the management of Gropius, Behne and Klein, those architects
who emphasized particularly the visionary and expressionistic approach came together. The organization
had on its main committee Otto Bartning, Bruno and Max Taut, and received support and interest from
Erich Mendelsohn, Bernhard Hoetger (from Worpswede) and Hermann Finsterlin, as well as Hans Poelzig,
Ludwig Hilberseimer and Hans and Wassili Luckhardt.

Under the chairmanship of Bruno Taut, the *Arbeitsrat* produced a pamphlet in December 1918, setting
out a six-point 'Architectural Programme' which sought to break down all existing barriers between the
arts. A new unity, the pamphlet warned, could only be achieved 'under the auspices of a new art of
building, in such a way that each separate discipline will contribute to it'. It goes on:

' . . . there will be no boundaries between the crafts, sculpture, and painting, all will be one:
Architecture. A building is the direct carrier of spiritual values, shaper of the sensibilities of the general
public which slumbers today but will awake tomorrow. Only a total revolution in the realm of the
spiritual can create this building; yet this revolution, this building, does not happen by itself. Both have
to be sought—today's architects must prepare the way for this edifice.'[4]

The first proposal put forward for action in the 'Programme' was for the design and construction of
Utopian buildings by 'radically inclined' architects supported by public funds. Experiment, vision,
architectural creativity and the organization of vigorous groups of like-minded individuals were the
other major proposals put forward in the 'Programme'.

Expressionist and Visionary architecture reached its peak, at least on paper, with the *Arbeitsrat*
'Exhibition of Unknown Architects' organized by Bruno Taut, Walter Gropius and Adolf Behne. This
was held at the gallery of J. B. Neumann in Berlin during April 1919. It was an exhibition that not only
offered the young creative architects an opportunity to display their visionary schemes but also
provided the general public with a consolidated point of view of an architectural future dominated by

Walter Gropius
c. 1925

*Wassili Luckhardt*

*Hans Luckhardt*

*Hans Scharoun*

*Hugo Häring*

66

what Walter Gropius defined in an exhibition pamphlet as the 'Cathedral of the Future' (*Zukunfts-kathedrale*). This echoed Taut's original programme that demanded a synthesis of the arts in which architecture, sculpture and painting were unified. In the pamphlet Gropius also attacked the folly of compromise solutions and demanded that the distinction between dream and reality should be clearly defined. In an apocalyptic vein he wrote:

'Architects, sculptors, painters, all of us must return to the crafts. For there *is* no art as a profession. Artists are craftsmen in the original sense of that word, and only in rare and divine moments of illumination, which lie beyond their own will-power, can art, unknowingly, burst into bloom from the work of their hands. You painters and sculptors should become craftsmen again; you should smash the frames of ''Salon Art'' that are around your paintings; go into the buildings, endow them with fairy tales of colour, engrave your ideas onto their naked walls—and *build in fantasy* without regard for technical difficulties. To have the gift of imagination is more important than all technology, which always adapts itself to man's creative will. Today there really does not exist a true architect, all of us are only the *forerunners* of the one who will some time again deserve to be called ''Architect'', a name signifying *Lord of Art*, who will make gardens of the desert and will heap wonders to the sky.'[5]

In the catalogue foreword to the exhibition Gropius wrote:

'All our works are no more than splinters; objects shaped by needs and utility cannot fulfil the longing for a fundamentally new world of beauty, for a rebirth of that spiritual unity which rose to the miracle of the Gothic cathedral. We shall not live to see it. But there is one consolation: the idea, the building-up of a white-hot, bold, far advancing idea which a happier time, bound to come, will realize.'[6]

The *Arbeitsrat* exhibition brought together not only adventurous architects but also graphic artists, painters and a Russian musician. The exhibits included drawings of architectural fantasies, watercolour sketches, plaster models and a painted tee-square hung up on nails. It was a display that showed coloured glass structures and fantastically shaped buildings the like of which had never been seen before; Hermann Finsterlin's globular structures were shown side by side with Taut's dreamworld of glass architecture and Paul Gösch's fairy-tale buildings. When the exhibition closed at Neumann's Gallery it then went the rounds of the working mens' bars of the Alexanderplatz.

During the same month that the *Arbeitsrat* exhibition was being held, Erich Mendelsohn's sketches were on show at Paul Cassirer's Berlin gallery, collected together under the title of 'Architecture in Steel and Concrete'. Also in the same month Gropius issued his *Bauhaus* Manifesto and found himself in a better position to bring to fruition the idea of a synthesis of the arts. He had taken up his appointment by the Provisional German Government as Director of the two existing Weimar establishments, the School of Applied Arts and the Academy under the restyled title of the *Staatliches Bauhaus, Weimar*. This move turned Gropius's idea into reality as the *Bauhaus* was 'inaugurated with the specific object of realizing a modern architectonic art, which, like human nature, should be all-embracing in its scope'.

To carry out his task Gropius drew to the *Bauhaus* many of the Expressionist artists whom he had come into contact with in the revolutionary art groups both pre and postwar. Expressionist painters such as

Klee, Kandinsky and Feininger found a true home in the experimental teaching atmosphere of the *Bauhaus* and provided the place with that 'spiritual counterpoint' that Gropius desired.

During the period of intense activity in the spring of 1919, the *Arbeitsrat für Kunst* addressed a number of questions to its members in an attempt to find out if there was any common point of view and in order 'to clarify the position of the artists in relation to the tendencies of the time'. The questions were answered by fifty leading artists, architects and critics and published in the first book of the *Arbeitsrat* under the title of *Ja! Stimmen des Arbeitsrates für Kunst in Berlin* (Yes, Opinions of the Arbeitsrat für Kunst in Berlin).

The single idea that emerged from the contributions to the book was the desire to create a Utopia: 'Let us then live in Utopia,' Hermann Obrist wrote, 'let us fabricate plans, castles in Spain; let us pretend and let us prepare for the time that will come thirty years hence, when Germany will triumphantly lead in the arts. . . . I have completely given up this calling—that is, sculpture—and I design, in solitude, fantasies (painted and drawn) which, I think, go well beyond the so-called Expressionist.'[7]

The Utopian dream, which resulted in the production of the wild paper fantasies, was reinforced by the lack of building opportunity. It was possible to dream and scheme but not to work for real clients with

*Bruno Taut:* Haus des Himmels

*Cover of the first publication of the* Arbeitsrat für Kunst

*Max Taut:* Das Drehbare Haus, *1921*

the money and materials to carry out actual work; it was a time in which to exchange ideas and discuss purely aesthetic questions.

Bruno Taut, the master mind of the 'Utopians', had begun an informal chain letter association with other members of the *Arbeitsrat für Kunst* in November 1919 thereby replacing the open official programmes previously issued by the Council. This 'Utopian Correspondence' as it became known, linked the fourteen participants of *Die gläserne Kette* (the Glass Chain) from the date of Taut's first circular of 24 November 1919 until Hermann Finsterlin's last contribution of 24 December 1920.

This correspondence was in most cases used by Taut as material for his publication *Frühlicht* (first series) and in order to preserve the anonymity of the contributors, because of the generally very tenuous and speculative nature of the group, most of the participants in the 'Utopian Correspondence' assumed pseudonyms. Carl Krayl (Tuttlingen) was known as Anfang; Hans Scharoun (Insterburg)—Hannes; Walter Gropius (Weimar)—Mass; Jakobus Göttel (Cologne)—Stellarius; Hans Hansen (Cologne)—Antischmitz; Wilhelm August Hablik (Itzehoe)—W. H.; Wilhelm Brückmann (Emden)—Berxbach 7; Hermann Finsterlin (Stuttgart)—Prometh. Of the Berliners Wassili Luckhardt was known as Zacken; Hans Luckhardt—Angkor; Paul Gösch—Tancred; characteristically Bruno Taut was known as 'Glas' while his essentially practical brother risked the use of his own name.

The controversial nature of some of the contributions that were reproduced in Taut's *Frühlicht* eventually caused the editors of *Stadtbaukunst alter und neuer Zeit,* who were responsible for its publication as a supplement to their magazine, to withdraw their support. Gurlitt particularly, found Paul Gösch's

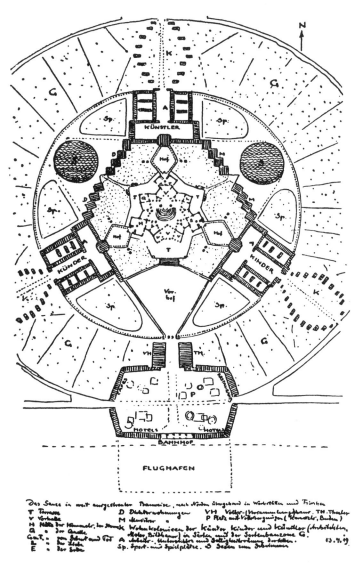

Bruno Taut: *the layout of the* Haus des Himmels

Above right: *Carl Krayl: the cathedral of Christian Science*

Right: *Paul Gösch: a study for a foyer*

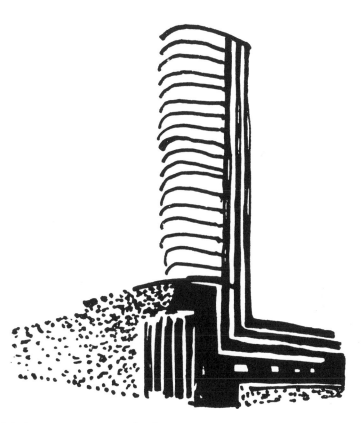

*Study for the* Chicago Tribune *Tower
by Hans Scharoun*

article 'Anregungen' quite intolerable, and with its appearance in the fourteenth issue an editorial statement was also included that announced the end of the Berlin *Frühlicht*.

Through Taut's *Frühlicht* the work of the visionary architects became known and before the end of its Magdeburg run Scharoun, Mendelsohn, Krayl, Söder, Gropius and Mies van der Rohe had all had representative projects shown in its pages. Wassili and Hans Luckhardt displayed an interest fairly early on in 1919 in sharp angular shaped formplays, and these appeared in the first issues of *Frühlicht* in 1920. They also produced imaginary projects for theatre buildings, cultural halls as well as graphic 'odes to joy'. With the interval of vision and fantasy over, in 1923–4, their work became rectangular and blocky with a strong emphasis on such motifs as the horizontal bands of windows and under-cill panels. But even then, with such a concern for the purity of rectangular shapes, the Luckhardt brothers felt free to explore occasionally the possibilities of free curved façades. This can be seen in the Telschow-House, built on the Potsdamer Platz, Berlin, in 1929 (in collaboration with Alfons Anker) and in their winning entry for the Alexanderplatz competition of the same year.[8]

It was during the Expressionist phase that Otto Bartning put out a plea for a new church architecture. In 1919 he published his *Von Neuen Kirchenbau* and in 1921 showed his Expressionist interest in church architecture with his model for a *Sternkirche*.[9] Internally this church had a similarity to the chapel projected by Gaudí for the Colonia Güell (1898–1915), although it is more consistently organized on

71

*Utopian sketch by Hans Scharoun, 1920*

72

*Otto Bartning: the Sternkirche, 1921.
Plan and section*

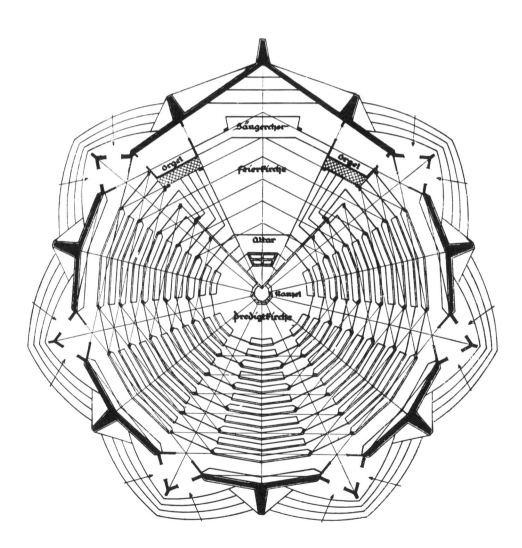

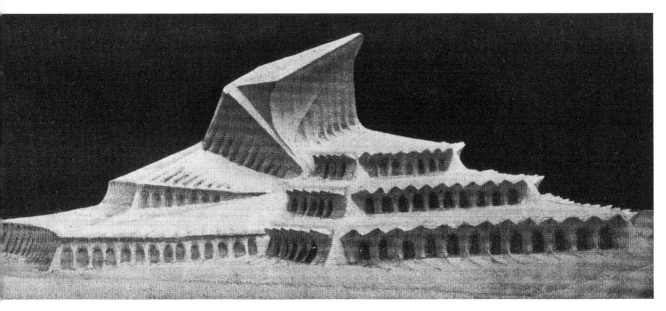

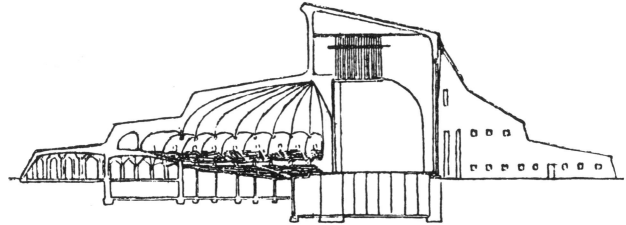

*Wassili and Hans Luckhardt: model for a people's theatre, 1922, and a section*

Upper left: *Wassili and Hans Luckhardt, Telschow House, Potsdam Square, Berlin, 1929*

Upper right: *Wassili and Hans Luckhardt, House of Culture*

Lower: *Wassili and Hans Luckhardt, form fantasy, 1919*

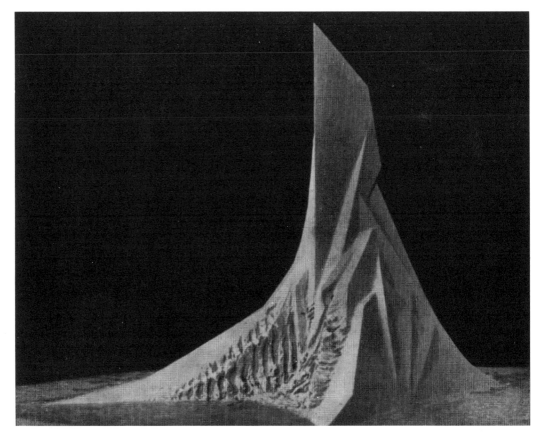

Hans Scharoun: the head of the
bridge, Cologne, 1926

Hans Scharoun: Skyscraper project,
Friedrichstrasse, Berlin, 1921

76

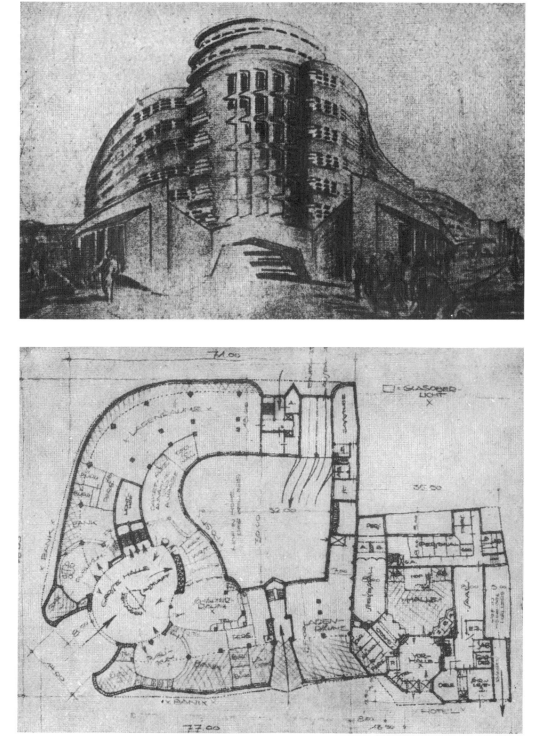

*Hans Scharoun:
Competition entry,
office and
commercial
building, Königs-
berg, 1921.
Sketch perspective
and plan*

77

*Hugo Häring: farm buildings at Gut Garkau near Lübeck, 1923–4. The Cow House, and a general plan*

Key to plan

A Farmhouse

B Barn

C Pigsty

D Stable

E Cowhouse

F Dunghill

G Cart and storage shed

H Chicken house

J Lake

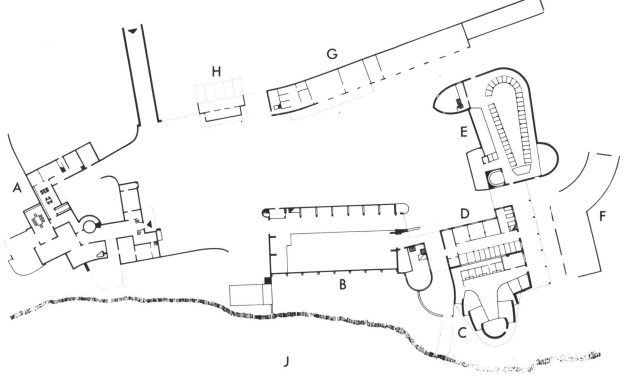

plan, and has a faceted exterior that is only made possible by a very complex parabolic structure of interlocking columns which act as supporting beams for the eyebrow shaped clerestory windows.

Expressionist architecture began on paper and remained there for many architects. For some it produced a conviction that architecture was primarily concerned with shaping the outward form of a building from a well organized plan. This new spatial and form-giving attitude is still common and valid today in the work of an architect like Hans Scharoun. The true architectural value of this approach however is best seen in the work of Hugo Häring in the group of farm buildings he designed for Gut Garkau near Lübeck, in 1923–4. These buildings (which Jürgen Joedicke first brought to the notice of our own generation), together with the Luckenwalde Hat Factory by Mendelsohn, demonstrate something of the aesthetic validity of a more intuitive approach to design.

The buildings for the farm at Gut Garkau, are the key to the work of a masterful designer, which is comparable in spirit to the later work of Alvar Aalto in Finland.

Joedicke in his article 'Häring at Garkau', published in the *Architectural Review* in May 1960, summarized Hugo Häring's standpoint:

'(Häring) explains that the renewal of architecture would have to take place in two stages. The first stage would have to deal with an exploration of the changed requirements of the time and would aim at functional efficiency. Häring uses the word *Organwerk*, "the task of developing the architectural organism". The second stage deals with the *Gestaltwerk*, the task of finding an adequate architectural expression or image.'[10]

One of Häring's basic maxims was that the architectural image can only be discovered through a study of function. 'We want to examine things and allow them to discover their own images. It goes against the grain with us to bestow form on them from the outside, or to impose some abstract modular upon them. . . .'[11]

Mies van der Rohe, Walter Gropius and Ludwig Hilberseimer, later advocates of an extremely rational and socially-minded approach to the problems of architecture, were all involved in this interval of fantasy. Mies particularly, before coming under the purging influence of Theo van Doesburg's cubistic *de Stijl* movement, mixed the soft world of coloured glass and the free plan with the precise world of the new technology. Even as late as 1929, when he had become one of the leaders of the *Neue Sachlichkeit* approach, he added a touch of romanticism to his otherwise purely functional Barcelona *Werkbund* Pavilion. Here the bold calculated effect of placing within the cold technological framework of the Pavilion a touch of warmth, with a piece of sculpture by Kolbe (which was to be viewed through tinted glass) suggests something of his earlier, clearly visionary phase. That short visionary interval is best seen in his various skyscraper projects.

The first of the office projects was designed in 1919 and was for a competition held to develop the Friedrichstrasse station site in Berlin. Mies saw here an opportunity to come to terms with the new material—glass. 'We see,' he wrote at that time, 'the new structural principles most clearly when we use glass in place of the outer walls, which is feasible today since in skeleton building these outer walls

Mies van der
Rohe: Glass sky-
scraper, 1920–1.
Model

do not actually carry weight. The use of glass imposes new solutions.'[12]

In the Friedrichstrasse project he goes on to say, he designed a building of 'prismatic form' for the triangular site and 'placed the glass walls at slight angles to each other to avoid the monotony of over-large glass surfaces.'[13] There is a logic behind these projects of Mies's that is not found in the work of other architects at that time. Even the curves of the plan of his second Expressionistic skyscraper block of 1920–1 are excused from any arbitrariness by the fact that they were 'determined by three factors: sufficient illumination of the interior, the massing of the building viewed from the street, and lastly the play of reflections'.[14]

The office building of 1922, with its rigid horizontal planes of reinforced concrete alternating with bands of horizontal windows shows Mies's architecture stripped of all overtones of style and decoration, depending for its effect on the simplification of structure. It is this attitude of the 'Maximum effect with minimum means' that clearly cuts him off from his contemporaries.[15]

It has been suggested that the monument to the Communists Rosa Luxemburg and Karl Liebknecht (1926) displays Expressionist tendencies. But this memorial, when seen in relation to the other brick buildings Mies was occupied with during the years 1925–9, clearly owes its origin to the popularity at that time of Frank Lloyd Wright's domestic architecture, and to the use of Dutch Elementarist ideas. Indeed, the whole design is in the form of a *de Stijl* composition, a bulky three-dimensional brickwork canvas which has a blank back wall.

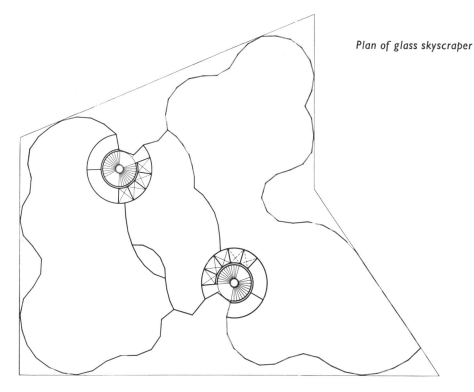

*Plan of glass skyscraper*

Walter Gropius's Expressionist interests were displayed not only in his first postwar construction, the Weimar monument (1920), but also in the two houses he built in Berlin—the Sommerfeld House (1921–2) at Berlin-Dahlem, and the house for Dr Otte at Berlin-Zehlendorf (1922). These houses were in fact quite unlike each other, and quite unlike anything that Gropius built later.

The Sommerfeld House was constructed of timber with the interior surface woodwork cut and carved in angular patterns: much of this work having been done by students of the Weimar *Bauhaus*. The designs being produced by Johannes Itten in the *Bauhaus* Basic Course at that time bear a distinct relationship to this kind of interior wood carving, but where the original inspiration came from is difficult to decide. The Otte house, which can be compared to Bartning's Wyleberg House, is less sensational than the Sommerfeld, but the sharp angularity of the front canopy and the cut-back of the dormer window indicates a freer architectural vocabulary that has little to do with Gropius's later functionalist aesthetic.

By 1924, the same group of architects who had come together in the *Novembergruppe*, with a number of notable additions, had formed a new organization called the 'Circle of Ten' which again a year later broadened out and was renamed 'The Ring'. It included within its membership as well as those mentioned before (excluding Finsterlin and Hoetger) Mies van der Rohe, Ernst May, Peter Behrens, Heinrich Tessenow, Richard Döcker, Hans Scharoun, Arthur Korn and Heinrich Lauterbach. Hugo Häring was the first secretary of the new association. In these new groups, as Joedicke has pointed out, 'the names of the members are sufficient indication of the strongly divergent opinions, and while there was mutual tolerance and forebearing, there could be no unified policy. The only common ground between these men was the search for a new way and the fight against retrogressive movements.'[16]

In the immediate postwar groups the architectural 'dreamers' met the architects who strongly advocated a new technological approach. Later, when Mies van der Rohe took over the leadership of the 'Ring', the Expressionist interest had waned and a more rational, technologically based, rectilinear architecture became more acceptable to the designers in the association. By 1927 the *Werkbund* exhibition at Stuttgart which was erected under Mies's direction showed the complete victory of the *Neue Sachlichkeit* approach. All the buildings were rectangular and cleanly shaped, and even such powerful ex-Expressionists as Poelzig, Taut and Scharoun toed the functional line. In not inviting Mendelsohn to construct a building at the Stuttgart exhibition, Mies made his own position very clear; it was also an omission that caused a rift in their friendship.

The more conservative work of the architects outside Berlin shows a deeper concern for the eccentric angularity of Expressionist-type forms.

Fritz Höger's *Chilehaus*, built in Hamburg in 1923, is probably the best known Expressionist type of building outside Berlin. This vast brick office block curves around its site and ends up sharply at the street corner, like the prow of an enormous ship. In this building as well as in the building in Hanover for the offices of the *Hannover Anzeiger* (1928) Höger stressed the use of vertical brickwork—a common feature of the work of the more traditional Expressionist architects.

*Fritz Höger: Chile House, Hamburg, 1923*

*Edmund Meurin: Boiler House,*
*Königsberg, 1922–3*

The buildings of Wilhelm Kreis which have an affinity to the work of Höger, if not the same kind of spirit, do not fit so comfortably into the Expressionist phase; although Kreis emphasized the vertical use of brickwork for his supporting members in the vast circular *Rheinhalle* (Planetarium) built at Düsseldorf in 1926. Here also the other exhibition buildings for the *Gesolei* are made up of a strange combination of Dutch brickwork treatment and what looks like pseudo-Egyptian detailing.

At Bremen, the sculptor-architect Bernhard Hoetger built the Expressionistic Paula Modersohn-Becker Haus (now rebuilt) erected on the famous Böttcherstrasse, which exploited the eccentric use of brickwork detailing to the full. It is probably the nearest the Germans ever got to the Dutch *Wendingen* brickwork style; in fact it clearly outdid anything that de Klerk or Kramer could have done by its sheer eccentricity. In this scheme too, the treatment of the iron-work railings was obviously derived from some *Jugendstil* source.

Many examples can be given of buildings bearing an Expressionist touch in Germany in the years up until the thirties, as diverse as Edmund Meurin's Boiler House at Königsberg of 1922–3 and Emanuel Josef Margold's work in Berlin. Other examples can be seen in such books as Hajos and Zahn's *Berliner Architektur der Nachkriegszeit* and the *Deutsche Baukunst der Gegenwart* series edited by Walter Müller-Wulckow, which clearly illustrate the transition from vision to practice in the architecture of Germany during the first ten years after the war.[17] It was a transition during which the paper and plaster model projects and the few austere postwar schemes were replaced by a prosperous and vital architectural situation that was only to be halted some few years later by the retrogressive demands of the Nazi regime and the appearance of the National Socialist architectural style.

# 7

Im Stil ist das Spiel das Ziel
Im Spiel ist das Ziel der Stil
Am Ziel ist das Spiel der Stil
*Paul Scheerbart*

# Bruno Taut and *Glasarchitektur*

While both Hans Poelzig and Peter Behrens sought for new qualities of architectural form, Bruno Taut (1880–1938) in the years immediately prior to the Great War was experimenting with the architectural potential of new materials. In his use of glass, concrete and steel he was also concerned with early ideas for the prefabrication of building elements.

Taut began his career as a mason but later studied architecture under Theodor Fischer at Stuttgart. He started a practice in Berlin before the war. Although many of his ideas for a new 'visionary' architecture were developed during the war years it was not until after 1918 that they were published. With the war over his importance as a leader of the architectural debate in the confused and war-wearied Germany became clear. His personality dominated many of the revolutionary groups that had mushroomed in postwar Berlin and he was responsible, as signatory, for the six-point 'Architectural Programme' issued by the newly formed *Arbeitsrat für Kunst* at Christmas 1918. In April 1919 the *Arbeitsrat* 'Exhibition for Unknown Architects' was arranged (this has been dealt with in greater detail in Chapter 6), and it was mainly to the contributors to this exhibition that Taut circularized his letter which formed the basis of the so-called 'Utopian Correspondence', later referred to as the 'Glass Chain' and probably the most significant exchange of theoretical ideas on architecture this century.

As Founder and Editor of the magazine *Frühlicht* ('Dawnlight') and as the prolific writer of books on architectural subjects, as well as a practitioner of no mean reputation in Germany during the twenties, Taut was in the forefront of the apologists of the new movement in architecture. However, it is Taut the visionary we are dealing with in this chapter, and it is necessary straight away to indicate his connections with his master, Paul Scheerbart (1863–1915), the Expressionist poet and novelist who was a fringe member of Herwarth Walden's *Sturm* circle. The relation of Taut to Scheerbart and the Expressionists is in many ways analogous to that of Sant 'Elia with Marinetti and the Futurists.

Taut's friendship and admiration for the older 'astral phantast' Scheerbart resulted in two related works: Taut's Glass Pavilion, erected for two German glass manufacturers at the 1914 Werkbund Exhibition at Cologne, and Scheerbart's publication *Glasarchitektur*. The interaction of these two works is evident, but

Bruno Taut, above

Max Taut

*Paul Scheerbart. A drawing by Oskar Kokoschka*

since both appeared in the same year a dispute has existed as to which was the source and which derivative. Certainly in his previous novels Scheerbart had depicted the world of glass and colour that Taut attempted to capture in the Pavilion. Scheerbart dedicated his book to Taut; while on the outside of the Pavilion, forming their own dedication, the phrases that Scheerbart wrote especially for Bruno Taut are prominently displayed: 'Coloured glass destroys hatred'; 'Without a glass palace life is a burden'; 'Glass brings us a new era, building in brick only does us harm', etc.[1]

'The *Glashaus*' Taut wrote at the time of its opening 'has no other purpose than to be beautiful.' It was a glass building throughout, glass walls—glass prisms in a concrete frame—glass doors, and glass staircases. The building was erected on a curved concrete apron and was basically a space frame dome resting on a fourteen-sided drum of glass bricks. On the string-course between the drum and dome were inscribed the Scheerbart aphorisms. The formal entrance staircase cut into the concrete podium (cf. the entrance to Mendelsohn's Einstein Tower, 1919–21) and led into the lower part of the building and to the sparkling water cascade that formed the central feature of the building. The polychromatic interior was divided in two at the base of the dome, the upper portion being entered from the staircases on either side of the building. The dome itself was many-faceted, each one of its rhomboid shapes filled in with Luxfer prisms faced on the inside with coloured glass and on the outside with clear plateglass panes. The total effect was heightened internally by a kaleidoscope that threw its coloured light on the running water, and by the translucence of the paintings on glass that were let into the wall surface; these paintings were based on designs by Jan Thorn-Prikker, Max Pechstein, Emanuel Josef Margold and Fritz Bekker.

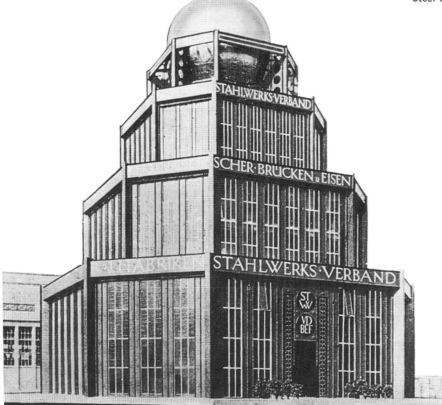

In Scheerbart's prophetic words and through the genesis of the 'glass paradise' in Taut's designs the important concept of removing the limits of solid walls to allow complete freedom of 'inner' and 'outer' space evolved.

'If we wish to raise our culture to a higher plane,' Scheerbart wrote in *Glasarchitektur* ,'then we are compelled, for better or worse, to change our architecture and this will only be possible for us when we remove the boundaries from the rooms we inhabit. We can however only achieve this by the introduction of glass architecture which lets the light of the sun and the moon and the stars into the room, not only through the windows—but through as many walls as possible that are completely of glass—of coloured panes. The atmosphere which we thereby create for ourselves must bring us a new culture.'[2]

Besides extending these revolutionary ideas into practice, Taut's little Pavilion at the Cologne Exhibition was an advertisement for a modern industry, just as its very interesting, but strangely insignificant-looking predecessor, the *Monument des Eisens* had been. This little building was designed a year previously by Taut in collaboration with Franz Hoffmann as a symbol of the Steel Industry, and it was erected for the 1913 Leipzig Fair. The size and external appearance of these structures belied their true importance as two of the most advanced buildings in the world at that time.

Glass Pavilion, Cologne, 1914

Interior of Glass Pavilion. Ground floor

Right: *Entry for the House of Friendship Competition, Istanbul, 1917*

Apart from the originality displayed in these two prewar structures, it was during the immediate post-war period that Taut, through his writing and sketches, began to explore the visionary aspects of architecture. In his literary style he obviously still owed a great deal to Paul Scheerbart (who died in October 1915), even though his circle of contacts in the postwar cliques had grown much wider and represented many divergent points of view. Through the pages of his magazine *Frühlicht* Taut and his colleagues continually stressed ideas for a new society as well as those for a new architecture; they wished to reshape the very earth itself.

In spite of the fact that many of Taut's ideas were wildly impracticable, a characteristic that has almost always been common to projects of a Utopian kind, he was not an impractical architect by nature as one can see from the detail aspects of his designs. He was, to quote Hermann Scheffauer's description, 'a visionary in practice'. It was during the war years, when practice was impossible, that Taut's vision for an 'Alpine Architecture' was drawn up. His designs, published in book form in Hagen in 1919 under the title *Alpine Architektur*, were certainly technologically impossible to execute as well as being economically impracticable, but this should not deter us from admiring the audacity of the concept. The magnificent water-colour drawings, with their poetic annotations, had a power all of their own. In Taut's dream world for the Alps, mountains and valleys were transformed into vast spatial cities surmounted by filigree structures in concrete and coloured glass; lakes were to be dammed to provide power as well as pleasure and amenity, and terraces faceted into the sides of the mountains. Glass again was to be used as the primary building material. In commenting on the idea Scheffauer wrote in the *Architectural Review*

90

in 1922: 'We have the dreams of a demiurge—nothing less than plans for rebuilding the planet, beginning with the Alpine villages, slopes and peaks.' Taut sought to create the architecture for the Alps through forms that would have universal spatial validity and a timeless quality. Mountain peaks were to be accentuated by a single giant crystal dome structure dedicated to music and contemplation, and this was to be surrounded by tier upon tier of ancillary glass buildings. In this environment man would live, work and play, experiencing a new sense of freedom among the *Farbenlichten*. Taut closes his book with a poetic declaration 'to reach for the stars'—the stars that would be viewed each night from the interior of his crystal houses.

In 1919 Taut also collected and published a number of essays under the title *Die Stadtkrone* ('The City Crown') which were mainly concerned with the development of a dominant central element in town planning. In the book, contributions were included from Erich Baron, Adolf Behne and from the writings of the late Paul Scheerbart. In his own essay Taut puts forward his arguments for the creation of a focal building around which the various elements of a town could be grouped; a huge crystal house through which the traditions, cultural and social achievements, and the aspirations of a city could be expressed. His own Cologne Glass Pavilion served as a prototype in miniature. Taut traced the importance of the 'city crown' in previous cultures, and drew upon examples of *Alter Stadtbekrönungen* from such diverse places as Mont Saint-Michel, Strasbourg, Durham, Angkor Vat and Bangkok to prove his point. He

sensed the danger of modern society erecting its new cities and towns without this essential binding-in element of the 'city crown' and producing a *'Rumpf ohne Kopf'*—a body without a head. Almost simultaneously with the publication of Taut's essay the first example of a giant glass 'city crown' structure appeared, not however from his drawing board but from that of Mies van der Rohe.[3] And it is to Mies that the credit must go for extending the world of the glass dream, after an initial interest in playful forms, into the rigid confines of trabeation.

In *Alpine Architektur* and *Die Stadtkrone* Taut was dealing with the age-old problem of the creation of an Ideal City as well as with the promotion of a visionary architecture on a large and complex scale. He examined the city in terms of its Utopian form, its overall organizational structure and morphology, thus bringing into focus the concept of the revolutionary new city which renounced simple utilitarian ideas, and came under the imaginative control of a *Weltbaumeister*, a 'master of world architecture'.

In his next book *Die Auflösung der Städte* (The Dissolution of the Cities), 1920, which was a less ambitious volume than *Alpine Architektur* but illustrated and annotated in the same fantastic style, Taut cries out against the congestion and chaos of the existing environment in the great cities. It appears that his cries

*Max Taut: watercolour study*

*Max Taut: Wissinger tomb, 1920*

Bruno Taut's Tribune Tower entry, Chicago, 1922. The project—which did not receive an award—was based on a square plan out of which the bell-shaped structure grew up to a point. Unfortunately the site itself was not square, so a smaller block at the rear also had to be provided[3]

KRISTALL HAUS UND HOF DER NEUEN SCHULE

*Bruno Taut: Crystal House*

*Max Taut: Marble Cathedral*

94

were heard at least in one grey conservative city in Germany. In 1921 Taut was appointed City Planner and architectural adviser to the old city of Magdeburg and immediately he began the revitalization of its decaying core. He introduced, to a storm of protest from the local citizens, his ideas for a chromatic architecture and the consistent use of colour on the façades of indistinguished buildings as well as the design of a number of very original structures, including a vast business house, a *Halle für Stadt und Land*, a festival hall and a war monument.

After his move to Magdeburg, Taut continued his publishing activities and reorganized his magazine *Frühlicht* in the autumn of 1921 as a separate publication. Before then it had appeared as a supplement to the Berlin periodical *Stadtbaukunst alter und neuer Zeit* which was edited by Cornelius Gurlitt, Bruno Möhring and Taut himself. It was included with fourteen of the fortnightly editions of the parent magazine from January to July 1920. The Berlin *Frühlicht* presented the radical viewpoint of the 'Utopians' and included contributions from Behne, Finsterlin, Gösch, Bommersheim as well as the inevitable extracts from Scheerbart. It was illustrated throughout by expressionist black and white drawings of the 'Glass Chain' group, Bruno and Max Taut, Scharoun, Finsterlin, Krayl, Gösch and Hans and Wassili Luckhardt.

In the four Magdeburg editions, from Autumn 1921 to Summer 1922, the magazine took on a more international flavour and while still continuing to feature the hypothetical and exploratory articles and drawings of the 'Glass Chain' it included side by side with this work actual building schemes (mainly by Taut for Magdeburg), a number of Constructivist projects from Russia (including Tatlin's monument for the Third International) and an article by J. J. P. Oud from Rotterdam.

Taut showed through his articles in *Frühlicht* an increasing interest in the problems of housing, particularly in the small individual dwelling which he referred to as a 'dwelling machine' (*Wohnmaschine, machine à habiter*). In an article in 1921 he produced various designs for a circular, beehive-type single family house, a modified prototype of which was exhibited in 1922 at the Central German Exhibition in Magdeburg. The idea of grouping single house units into formal and informal rows and shapes was also featured in *Frühlicht* and developed by Hans and Wassili Luckhardt and Theodor Grosse.

In 1923 Bruno Taut relinquished his post at Magdeburg and returned to Berlin to join his brother Max in private practice. Soon after that date Taut, then at the noonday of his architectural career, became fully occupied with current building projects and far more concerned (as his books on housing from 1924–7 show) with the practical and rational aspects of architecture.

By 1929 his position had been modified and he was able to demand in his book *Modern Architecture*, written for *The Studio* in England, that modern architecture should recognize:

'. . . no demarcations between façade and ground plan, road and courtyard or between the front and back of a building. Nor does any detail exist for its own purpose alone, but should be designed to serve as a necessary part in the general plan. Everything that functions well, looks well. We simply do not believe that anything can look unsightly and function well.'[4]

In contrast to his aesthetic speculation some ten years earlier, his demand at the close of the twenties was for a 'new movement' that required:

1. 'The uttermost utility' in a building.
2. Material and construction adopted to serve the above principle.
3. A definition of beauty, that 'originates from the direct relationship between building and purpose, from the natural qualities of the material and from elegance of construction.'

The simple thesis to be followed for a new aesthetic was that 'the aim of architecture is the creation of the perfect, and therefore also beautiful, efficiency'.[5]

# 8

Les fantaises apparentes du monde naturel ne
sont pas sans raison. Les structures naturelles
appraissant d'une logique de fonction implacable . . .
leur formation est dépendant d'une géométrie de
mouvement qui ne sacrifie jamais l'essentiel qui
est la vie, à l'absolu qui est une spéculation
inhumaine du nombre

*Jacques Couëlle*[1]

# Hermann Finsterlin and *Formspiel*

In many ways Hermann Finsterlin epitomizes the postwar revolutionary architect; he built nothing, yet became well known within the Utopian groups in Germany through his highly original sketches and unusual philosophical views on architecture.

Finsterlin was born in Munich in August 1887 which makes him one of the same generation as Erich Mendelsohn (born in the same year), Mies van der Rohe, Walter Gropius, Bruno Taut, Hugo Häring and the Luckhardt brothers. Unlike his contemporaries he was not a trained architect. His initial interest in the arts came, as Pevsner has pointed out, in true Expressionist fashion one moonlit night in 1910 when, at the top of a mountain in Bavaria, he 'saw in a flash that art was his vocation'. Previous to this experience he had studied chemistry, physics, medicine, philosophy and Indology. Since the moment of inspiration Finsterlin has dedicated his life to painting, sculpture and architectural speculation, and has exhibited his work in many European cities.

He first came to the notice of his contemporaries through the invitation from Walter Gropius to exhibit a number of architectural sketches in the *Arbeitsrat für Kunst* exhibition of 'Unknown Architects' in Berlin in 1919. On first sight these drawings, as far as the solution of tangible architectural problems were concerned, must have seemed more of a joke than a serious contribution to the aesthetics of a new architecture. They were in fact, even with all the wilful distortion of form they displayed, an extremely serious and remarkably consistent attempt to imbue architecture with life and a new richness of shape.

The designs were truly organic; a part of nature. A building for Finsterlin was to be a natural living organism; an idea that was quite different from Frank Lloyd Wright's concept of an 'organic' building designed 'in sympathy with nature'. In Finsterlin's work the tension and energy inherent in a building's enveloping materials—which in most cases meant concrete used like plasticine—were exploited plastically to form the skin and bones enclosing the habitable spaces. The interiors of his buildings were liberated from the restraints of right angles and became spacious caverns. Finsterlin put forward a plea for people to free themselves from the conventional confines of cubic living, from existing in a schematised interior.

*Hermann Finsterlin*

When describing an occupant's reaction to his concept of house interiors Finsterlin wrote: 'In the interior of the new house you will not only feel that you are an inhabitant of a fairy-tale crystallic gland but also a privileged inhabitant of an organism, wandering from organ to organ, a giving and receiving symbiont of a "gigantic fossilized parent body".'[2]

Through his fundamental and intuitive approach to architectural form Finsterlin sought to 'build for the earth', and felt he could derive little benefit from the work of other architects who were, as he says, 'too bound up in technical matters'. For Finsterlin a building was 'a work of all the arts together, a gigantic hollow sculpture with endless possibilities for exterior and interior shaping, with the sole requirement of aesthetic balance, of composition accurate to the last cubic centimetre even given the greatest complications'.[3]

Finsterlin's work has rested in obscurity for many years largely because it proved impossible to translate his architectural fantasies into actual buildings. This situation has changed considerably over the last ten years, and for many architects today Finsterlin's work has become a starting point for new ideas. Even now, though, with this revival of interest in his projects, he is little known in English-speaking circles, perhaps for the reason that it has proved almost as impossible to translate his very Expressionistic language into English as it was to translate his fantasies into architecture. In German, for example, his style has been referred to as a *'dithyrambisch-prometheischem-Zarathustra-Stil'*![4]

Through a process of careful elimination he stripped down the stylistic characteristics of architectural form into fundamental elements, developing side-by-side with this an original imagery of his own. In his projects too, as one would expect from a painter with strong affinities to the *Art Nouveau-Jugendstil*, the use of colour was carefully related to line and each contour had a harmonious place in the composition— whether the study is a small portrait sketch or an architectural formplay.

As the processes of time, technical skills, artistic invention and social and religious needs have contributed to the formation and refinement of architectural styles, nature too has, over millions of years, created her own forms and monuments by growth and erosion. It was these two principles that Finsterlin attempted to embody in his projects and sketches, the first with his *Baukasten der Welt-Architektur* (world architecture building blocks) and the second through his symbolic idea of a *Seelengletscher-mühlensystem*, a concept that is indeed virtually impossible to translate into English. The *Baukasten* were a set of small, shaped wooden blocks which could be built up into fundamental 'world architecture styles' as well as fantasies. The sets included blocks shaped as cubes, columns, pyramids, cones, half-spheres, domes, needles, onions, bells and horns. With these basic shapes it was possible to arrange them into various building types of all the major architectural styles; an Egyptian pyramid, a Greek temple, a Roman amphitheatre, a Romanesque and a Gothic church as well as oriental examples. The sets of blocks could also be split up to make any composition that took one's fantasy. The blocks naturally enough had a pedagogical purpose and were also designed with children in mind— they were patented and sold as 'a game of the styles' taken from 'all times and all nations'. A prospectus was issued to describe the scope and use as well as the architectural message of the building blocks, and

*Two ground plans, 1921 and 1925*

*Study for a house*

in this a number of examples were given of the various stylistic and fantasy compositions that could be assembled.

In an article, entitled 'The Genesis of World Architecture' in the third issue of the Magdeburg *Frühlicht*, Finsterlin described his building blocks as a tool for teaching, play and experiment and used them as models in an analysis of world architectural styles and a discussion of aesthetic values of lines, points, planes and solids. He distinguished three great epochs in world architecture:

a. *The coordinated epoch*, in which the primary elements of form were built up into complex three-dimensional and well proportioned structures.

b. *The geometrical and trigonometrical epoch*, in which the primary form elements were split up but combined in pairs and groups to form a well proportioned whole (e.g., a faceted dome).

c. *The organic epoch*, in which the intuitive use of hybrid forms created an 'incalculable organic fusion'.

Bautraum, *a house for the arts*

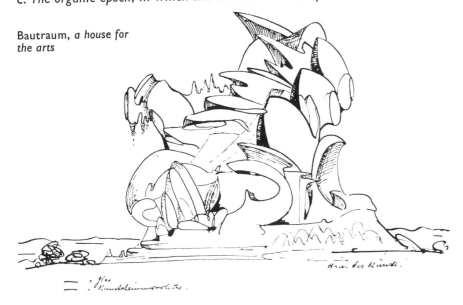

*The Play of Styles, building blocks, 1916*

*Free shapes out of building blocks*

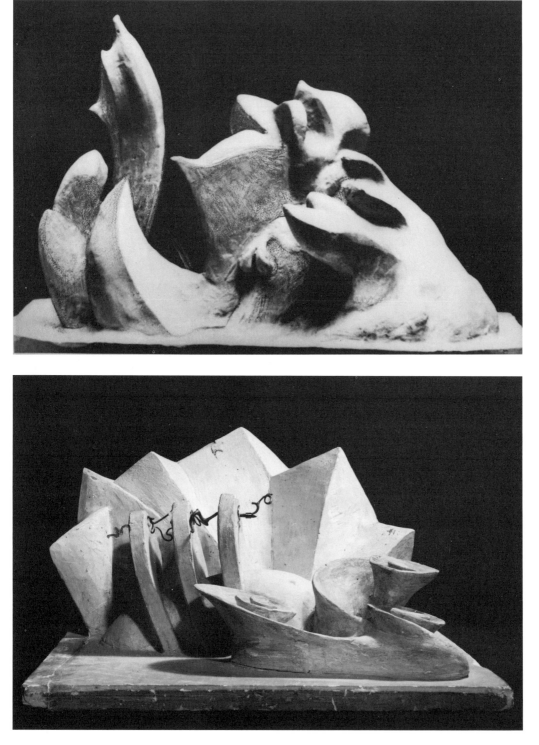

*The House of God, model, 1918*

*A mausoleum, model, 1919*

A guesthouse,
model, 1921

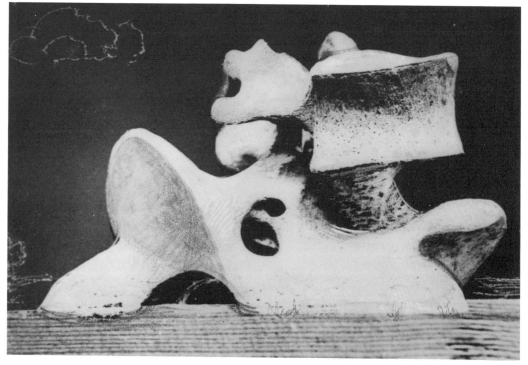

A clubhouse,
model, 1953

103

Rougerthaus, *1919*

For this article the building blocks were photographed to show the 'great folk styles' (i.e., clause a. above) while another page devoted to his characteristic sketches and called simply *Stilspiel* showed the development within the organic epoch (clause c).

It was largely through Taut's magazine *Frühlicht* and the 'Utopian Correspondence' he had initiated in 1919 that Finsterlin's ideas reached a wider public. At first Finsterlin was not keen to join in with Taut's anonymous group of correspondents—*Die Gläserne Kette*—mainly because he did not want to play hide-and-seek with the public. But to avoid being excluded from a group which otherwise appeared to be important to him he finally agreed to take part and to use a pseudonym. He chose the name 'Prometheus' (sometimes shortened to 'Prometh'), a title that stressed the contentious role he assumed in the group as an opposer, who could neither rank with the pure Expressionists and Utopians like Bruno Taut, Gösch and Krayl, nor with the 'all too practical men' like Max Taut, Häring, Hablik and Gropius. Finsterlin's most important contribution was an essay entitled '*Der achte Tag*' ('The Eighth Day') and this appeared under his own name in the eleventh part of the Berlin *Frühlicht*. In this essay Finsterlin expounded at length on his conception of a total building art:

'Building is everything, love, procreation, struggle, movement, suffering, parent and child, and the holiest symbol of all that is holy. I tell you such a built shape must sing like Memnon's granite body, when the sun's wide-awake glance caresses it. . . . And where the air is thinnest and shame melts before the purifying glance of the sun, a spectral building diamonds itself. . . .'[5]

104

*Cathedral, 1918*

*Study for model of the House of God, 1918*

*Study for a university, 1918*

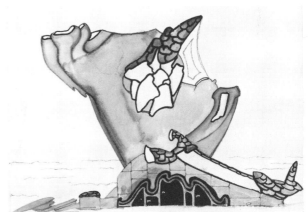

*Study for an exhibition room or a theatre, 1925*

*A technical high school, 1924*

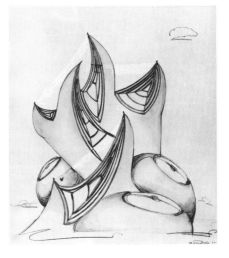

*Studio house, 1925*

He goes on in this vein of fantasy to describe the effects of the new building art on 'ephemeral beings' and of its purifying influence on the soul of man. Architecture, he wrote, 'is a biogenetic phenomenon of the human essence which lies beyond the foetal'. In the same article he attacks the perpendicular nature of the work of the more practical, rational architects. His own idea of what architecture should be is shown in the sketches that accompany the article and which are described as 'gloriously shaped organisms' that could rise out of the use of new materials and forms.

Finsterlin's concept of a *Seelengletscher-mühlensystem* was derived directly from a geological source, from the well-known example of glacial erosion in Lucerne and the caverns at Autring. *Gletschermühlen* are great stone hollows which have been shaped through millions of years by glacial water and in which fallen rocks have become rounded by constant movement within the hollow. It was the knowledge of this elementary, geological 'pestle and mortar' process that inspired the craggy appearance and timeless quality of so many of Finsterlin's architectural models. In point of fact it became, as he says, 'his Symbol' for a new architecture, that would be close to nature and to the soul of man.

Finsterlin's dream world of organized architecture was as valid in its totality as Scheerbart and Taut's Glass Paradise and although it was a distinctly individual diversion back to paradise it was, and is, not without practical value. It is too easy to dismiss the *Formspielen* as just artists sketches of an imaginary world and the correspondence as pure art-talk, particularly if, as Blaauw pointed out in the special number of *Wendingen* on Finsterlin, any real architectonic value in the work is rejected because one sees in 'architecture the tight coalition of Man and Society as comprising all factors which make architectonic ideas into architecture'. It is the dreamers who, Blaauw continued:

'. . . must leave this world alone, which it must be admitted binds us with fetters, which darkens the mind's-eye. Let us accept Finsterlin's creations as architecture in the same way as we also accept our own boldest dreams as such . . . to see them wither and become rigid into ''buildings'' in the world of our reality. When we stay with Finsterlin in the wonderful world of his architectonic imagination, we shall be reminded of our boldest dreams, in which we thought ourselves free from past and present, and then when we return to our own architectural world, we shall perhaps carry along something of our own juvenile and almost forgotten dreams.'[6]

Unfortunately, and to a certain extent understandably, none of Finsterlin's projects were erected and one cannot assess, as one can with say, Mendelsohn's Einstein Tower, Steiner's Goetheanum buildings or even Le Corbusier's chapel at Ronchamp, whether he could have fully realized his ideas in practice. Although Finsterlin will remain with Antonio Sant 'Elia a paper visionary, there is an interesting postscript to his career and to the validity of his own ideas. With the growing interest in his work over the last few years it was only in 1962, at the retrospective exhibition of his drawings, paintings and models held at the Diogenes Gallery in Berlin, that he reiterated his demands for a truly modern architecture and firmly stood by his forty-year old convictions. He said:

'Most of you will have come here assuming at the age of seventy-five I have different, more mature, tamer or perhaps even negative relation to the ideas of my youth. The contrary is true. Today, after half a century I stand by these ideas, and the revived international interest of colleagues proves to me that the Glass Chain (as we called our young architects' society) was broken by the First World War, not by its own failing. . . . Should we not now, after the *Wirtschaftswunder* have a cultural miracle as well? There is something of the twenties in the Berlin of today. Not that I imagine that within a reasonable time Finsterlin cathedrals and houses will be built, but there is a longing for live play and greater richness of form. The technical progress of it should tempt us to make use of these magnificently widened possibilities in order to create a style for our time; which is architecture once more and not just building. To stimulate this I have kept my "fantastic architecture" on ice for so long.'[7]

*Erich Mendelsohn*

108

**9**

# Erich Mendelsohn and
# the architecture of dynamism

The contribution of Erich Mendelsohn to the development of modern architecture has been singularly important. The visionary aspect of his first designs, his concern for what he termed the 'continuity of architecture' and his philosophy of 'dynamics' and 'function' were the starting points for a life's work. This work, taken as a whole, defies classification and could most justifiably be called 'Mendelsohnism'. Mendelsohn was born in Allenstein, East Prussia, in 1887. The son of a merchant, it seemed that he was destined for a career in economics. Soon the creative lure of architecture became too strong for him and he gave up his studies in economics and turned to architecture. He trained first at Berlin, then moved to Munich in 1910 to study under the well-known architect and teacher, Theodor Fischer.

In Munich, the centre of the worn out *Jugendstil*, he was soon caught up in the prevalent revolutionary atmosphere of Expressionism. It was in Munich that the energetic and reactionary faction in the *Neue Künstler Vereinigung* under the leadership of Wassily Kandinsky broke from the traditionalism of the older artists in the Association and formed the *Blaue Reiter* group of artists in 1911–12.

The symbolistic and emotional emphasis in the work of the new painters formed a basis for Mendelsohn's own architectural credo, and their graphic work offered ideas for representation that he quickly assimilated into his own architecture. Indeed, his whole manner of design—working up an architectural idea from an expressionistic sketch—as well as his personal philosophy of 'Dynamism', demonstrated at a very early stage an attitude to design that was both idiosyncratic and brilliant; while his insight into the form problems of architecture remains unique.

Mendelsohn drew directly on no historical models and his work during the formative years in the early twenties appears free from the stylistic overtones of many of his contemporaries. It was free from the eclecticism that still showed in the work of Hans Poelzig, which Mendelsohn admired so much, and free also from the overt visionary extravaganzas of people like Bruno Taut and Hermann Finsterlin.

In 1912 Mendelsohn began a small practice in Munich. But the war two years later curtailed its development, and Mendelsohn was soon called up to fight at the German front. It was during these war years that Mendelsohn committed his architectural ideas to paper and wrote his reflective words of wisdom on the meaning of architecture. These brilliantly lucid statements indicated Mendelsohn's attitude to architecture, at once clearheaded, exploratory and romantic. It was an attitude that was not to change in essence throughout his long and varied career. 'Architecture is the only tangible expression of space of which the human mind is capable,' he wrote in 1914. 'Architecture seizes upon space, encompasses space and is space itself.'[1]

Against this background of an architectural philosophy, the ideas he had for an architecture of 'dynamism' began; ideas which had their roots in the philosophy of Nietzsche and which provided inspirational drives to his architectural vision.

In an analysis of the architecture of Expressionism it becomes necessary to ask the question in what way were the buildings and paper-schemes intended to be Expressionistic?

In Mendelsohn's early works this is fairly easy to answer; he was trying to symbolize in modern technological terms the purpose of a building by its external forms, so that a factory for the production of cars in fact had something of the spirit of motion and streamlining in its shape, or a 'sacred building' something of the majesty and awe-inspiring qualities that one would associate with the Godhead. This was then, in architecture, an extension of the aims of the painters and writers to symbolize inner meanings of both physical life and human emotion in terms of form. It was Utopian in the sense that it ignored the reality of the situation in practical building terms. Mendelsohn attempted to create his symbolic architecture in mechanistic terms—similar in many ways to the Futurists—and not in terms of the organic naturalistic forms of his *Jugendstil* predecessors.

Sketch by sketch, Mendelsohn put together a drama of line and form that explored the plastic world of architectural symbols. The sketches themselves, executed in charcoal, ink, pencil or crayon, many of

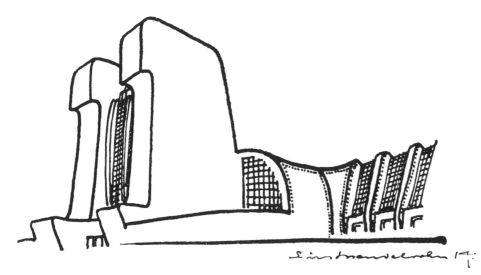

them little bigger than a matchbox top, were artist's drawings—expressionist drawings. In common with the artists' drawings of the time they were complete in themselves; each one telling a single story. It has become impossible to mention Mendelsohn's early work without reference to the general concept of Expressionism. Some critics have used the label exclusively to describe not only the sketches but also the whole of his German work. Mendelsohn himself would certainly not have accepted or welcomed the description used in that sense. As Arnold Whittick, Mendelsohn's biographer, has pointed out, 'There is a danger . . . of over-emphasising the influence of Expressionism' on Mendelsohn's work—the Italian critics Zevi and Roggero have tended to do this—and underestimating the later influences of Dutch and American work on his designs.

The case for an expressionist architecture was weakened for Mendelsohn by the difficulties encountered in the construction of the Einstein Tower. This experience seems to have forced him to adopt a more conventional rectilinear approach to architectural form. With the tower Mendelsohn reached the climax of his own expressionism. As his practice grew Mendelsohn's rejection of what had amounted to a literary and dramatic starting point for his architectural projects was reinforced by the essentially practical nature of his buildings.

Reyner Banham has summed this up in his definitive article on Mendelsohn in the *Architectural Review*: 'Like "Dr Mabuse", the last works of his German period seem, by implication, to reject Expressionism as the employment of the insane, and to substitute for it a more sensible and humane view of the world.'[2]

Mendelsohn's more sober attitude after the 'paper' (Impracticable Expressionist) phase, was reflected in a lecture he gave to the Amsterdam *Architectura et Amicitia* group in 1923. In this lecture, entitled 'The International Conformity of the New Architecture or Dynamics and Function', he spoke of the 'danger of uncontrolled temperament in dynamics' which corresponded 'to the equally great danger of too conscious an abstraction. Full-bloodedness and bloodlessness are both areas of danger for vital creation.' He continued, 'If the principle is considered to be an end in itself . . . then "the form *per se*" does not mean architecture. This is a law for all times, not only for Expressionism and Constructivism.'

Thus it was at about this time that the idea of a dynamic architecture became more closely allied to function and the free curves and fanciful nature of the earlier sketches gave way to blocky, rectilinear shapes based more often than not on feasible plans. But the earlier sketches are important, as it was with these that Mendelsohn freely explored the possibilities of plastic expression. 'I believe,' Mendelsohn wrote in 1955, 'that all original artists betray their individual significance in their first works—pregnant with new ideas—offering the best clue for everything that follows. For when the first idea is deep enough, life is too short to expound it fully.'[3]

No doubt if the building of the Einstein Tower had been easier, this kind of exploration would have continued. The sketches themselves only give a hint of what this architecture would have been like. With almost Wagnerian delight he produced schemes inspired by musical themes—charcoal *Agnus Dei*—graphic cathedrals dedicated to his God of music, J. S. Bach, as well as flippant cockleshell thumbnail sketches dedicated more appropriately to Bacchus. He used the sketch as a creative tool. Music, according to his former assistant Hans Schiller, he used 'as a physical convenience' while working, so that he could shut himself off from the outside world. As some people would draw a curtain to cut out the disturbing effects of strong sunlight, so Mendelsohn 'would surround himself with a "curtain" of music to shut out all disturbing outside influences which might keep him from concentrating on his creative task'.

Mendelsohn's work, as has been suggested earlier, does not lend itself easily to any kind of classification. He stands out rather, again to use the words of Hans Schiller, as a 'creative artist far ahead of his time', who 'formulated ideas of his own, prophetic of architecture to come', which 'technically partially accomplished in some works of the present-day architecture, still presages future developments'.[4] This prophetic characteristic reminds one of his Jewish nationality, and it certainly is a significant fact that many of his major patrons, both during his successful Berlin period and after his forced emigration, have been Jewish. One can feel in his writings a hint of a self-appointed Messianic purpose—to liberate architecture from the shackles of 'style' and plagiarism and to breathe into it a new, original, creative life.

At the beginning of his architectural career his original vision was moulded not only by the work of the Expressionist artists around him but also by the legacy of the *Jugendstil* and the influence of the 'arts and crafts' Sezession. He was very conscious of the forceful linear style that Henri van de Velde's least

talented followers had 'degraded into the marketable excrescence known now as ''Art Nouveau'' ' and at times, in the sketches of around 1914 for example, tried to put the style into its right perspective[5]. In an article in the *Architectural Review* Nikolaus Pevsner shows how close his link was to the Vienna Sezession circle; much closer than previous historians have allowed. Pevsner compares the preliminary drawing made by Olbrich for the Sezession building of 1898 with a drawing of 1914.[6] Two other drawings by Mendelsohn of 1914, both for 'Labour Halls', stress the link with Olbrich even more clearly, with the slablike forms of the sides of the building containing a large glazed area, under which is situated the entrance to the structure. The difference between the sketches is one of scale; the buildings indicated in Mendelsohn's sketches are monuments, while Olbrich's are conventionally scaled. Further links, particularly any with Sant 'Elia and the Futurists, are more difficult to find.

Mendelsohn's sketches themselves were to be, 'the criterion against which he would check all future development of the project'. The accuracy of the sketches in portraying the concept—even the finished building itself—is at times almost uncanny. Certainly it was through the sketches, particularly those for the Einstein Tower, that Mendelsohn's work was brought to the notice of the German public. Paul Cassirer, the Berlin publisher and art dealer, invited Mendelsohn to display some drawings at his gallery in an exhibition called 'Architecture in steel and concrete' late in 1919. The sketches were immediately derided by some critics as mere book illustrations, having little or no connection with real tangible architecture. What the critics failed to see was their true value and purpose as serious attempts at form exploration. The sketches, like his theoretical ideas, sought to 'recognize the elastic qualities of the new materials, steel and concrete', which Mendelsohn considered 'must by necessity produce an architecture entirely different from anything known before'.[7]

GROUND PLANS
+ 0 BASEMENT FLOOR. THE LABORATORY WITH MIRR-
ORS, ARC-LAMP, ELECTRIC OVEN, AND WALL FOR
DOUBLE-ACTION CAMERA, FIXED TEMPERATURE
ROOM WITH GRILLE AND PRISMATIC-SPECTROGRAPH.
ROOM FOR MICROPHOTOMETRICS, WITH ROOM FOR
STORAGE BATTERIES AND DARK-ROOM.
+ 3,39 ENTRANCE, STAIRCASE-HALL AND OFFICE.
+ 6,80 STAIRCASE-HALL, NIGHT QUARTERS.
+ 10,44 BASE FOR LENSES.
+ 14,45 BASE FOR CUPOLA WITH COELOSTAT.
+ 16,55 CUPOLA.

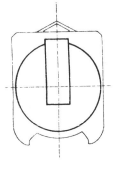

+16.55

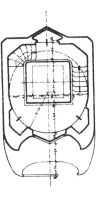

+14.45

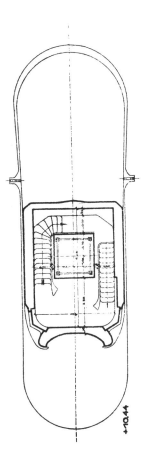

+10,44

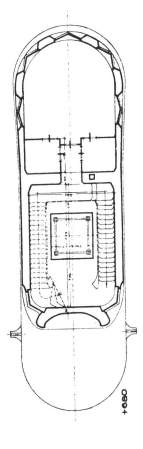

+6,80

114

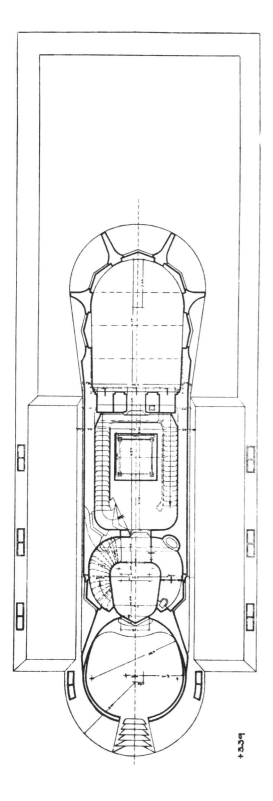

+ 3.39

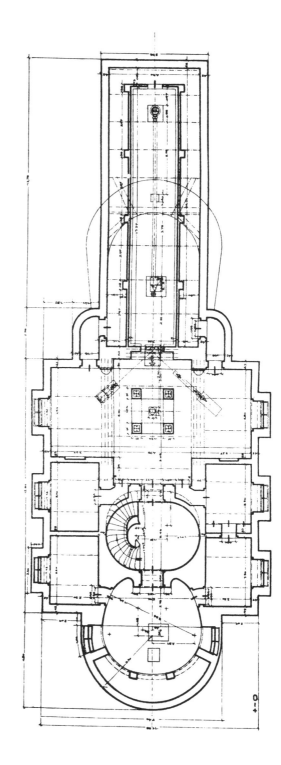

+ 1.0

*Floor plans of the Einstein Tower*

115

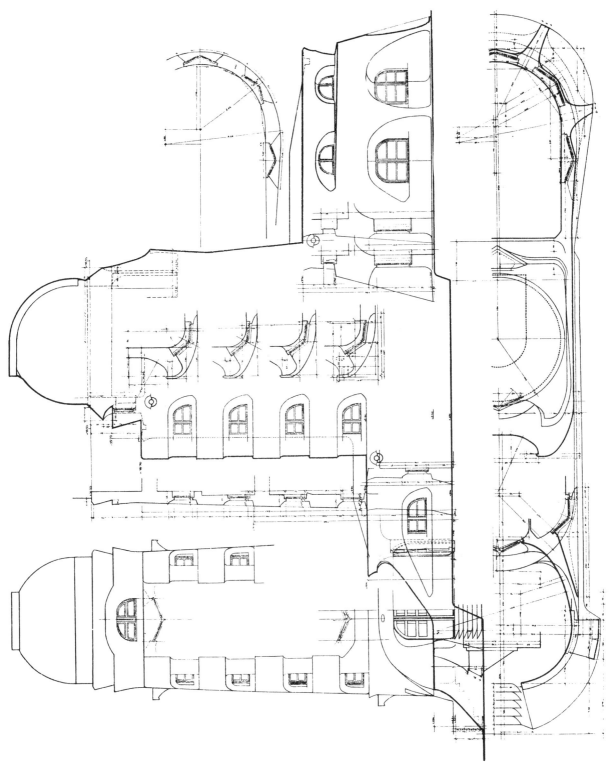

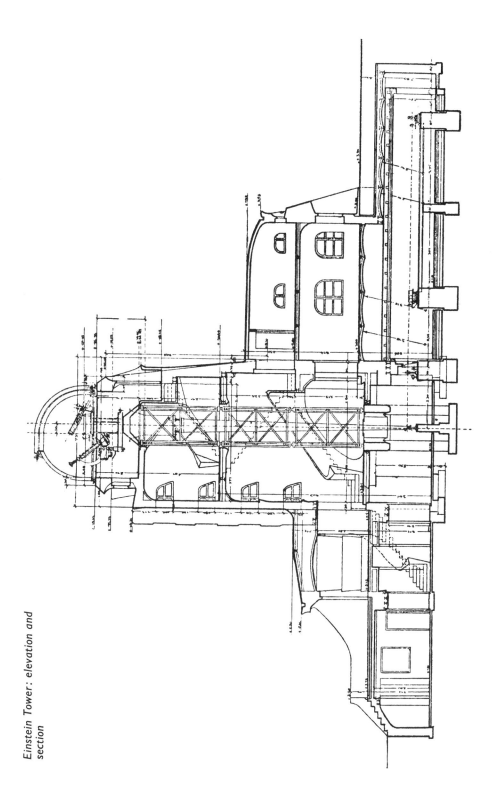

*Einstein Tower: elevation and section*

117

*Einstein Tower, Potsdam, 1920–1.*
*General view and detail of*
*entrance steps*

Reinforced concrete was Mendelsohn's material, its malleability his prime concern. This material, he felt, would give the range of forms and shapes necessary for the new architecture. It would also provide the break with the past; a break from the eclecticism that still pervaded much of the current work in Germany immediately before the war. Even during the time Mendelsohn was at Munich he had deplored the use of historical models, except possibly the Greek—which all German architects respected—and on more than one occasion openly rebelled against the form of teaching that included the assimilation of historical styles.[8] He saw his own work as a continuation of what he called 'creative resurgence', which he maintained could be found in three potentials, in the 'structural potential' of steel, indicated in the *Halle des Machines*, designed by Dutert and Contamin for the Paris Exhibition of 1889; in the 'form potential' of van de Velde's work at the Dresden Exhibition of 1906; and in the 'technical potential'—by which he meant the integration of material, construction and form—found in a structure such as the Railway Station, Hamburg of 1910.[9]

It was these potentials that Mendelsohn exploited with his Einstein Tower. The Einstein Tower still stands today at Potsdam as a monument to Mendelsohn's creative philosophy—the sarcophagus of Expressionism. It remains a monument as well to the whole corpus of sketches that occupied his hand and mind during the war years. It is an impressive structure, monolithic, symbolic and heavy, designed to simulate the grandeur of the Einsteinian concept. The development of the Tower to its final form can be clearly seen in the sketches that were begun as early as 1917, and which were completed with the actual Einstein project in hand in 1919. Through the sketches the dynamic possibilities of the building, begun as a simple observatory, were thoroughly explored. Unlike the work of his contemporary, Hermann Finsterlin, the form-player *par excellence*, who built nothing, the tower offered immediate practical architectural possibilities. Possibilities of form and structure which, although they could not be fully exploited at the time because of lack of certain building materials, were not taken up again until they were introduced much later in the work of architect engineers like Nervi, Torroja, Candela and Niemeyer; work which Mendelsohn himself said showed 'in structure and form (the) concept of elastic continuity envisioned in my early sketches'.[10] The plan of the Einstein Tower was axial throughout. The pistol-shaped basement plan at level O was designed to accommodate the main laboratory, the barrel portion of which housed the prismatic mirrors. The entrance hall was entered by a short flight of steps which led through a bowl-shaped space to the main staircase. The steel support for the coelostat rose up through the staircase to the cupola. The whole design had a functional clarity on plan and a spatial organization that was not too clearly expressed in the external forms of the building.

The Tower, as one of the key buildings of modern architecture, cannot be underestimated or over-looked, although it did receive more than its fair share of indignant comment soon after its completion. Indeed, Manning Robertson, when he referred to it in 1925 as 'a travesty of Einstein's contribution and a monument to complication and bewilderment', was reflecting pretty fairly the view of the conservative English architectural front at the time.[11] However, it is worth remembering that it was Einstein himself who whispered the word 'organic' into Mendelsohn's ear after visiting the completed structure.[12]

Mendelsohn said in his lecture to the Architectural Association in 1930: 'it must be admitted that the Einstein Tower is a real architectonic organism. It is at one and the same time an astrophysical institute built for the purpose of investigating Einstein's theory of relativity, and a monument to the scientist. Consequently it is not only a piece of architecture but something in the nature of a piece of sculpture as well.'[13]

The Tower more than any other of Mendelsohn's works best fulfils his conditions for a new architecture:

'The living quality of Architecture depends', he wrote, 'upon sensuous seizure by means of touch and sight: upon the terrestrial cohesion of mass, upon the super-terrestrial liberty of light. Out of its own laws Architecture lays down the conditions that govern its active masses: the dynamic condition—the movement of space—to visualize its linear elements by means of its contours; the rhythmic condition—to visualize the relation of the masses—by means of the projection of surfaces, and the static condition—the equalization of movement by means of the ground plan and section.'[14]

The overall shape of the Einstein Tower is dictated by this first condition of contour and movement. Its details, particularly the 'eye-brow' projections above the windows, which cut and project into the main surface, fulfil the second condition of rhythm, while the third condition, the static, is found in the plans taken at different levels throughout the building, in the section and in the axial layout.

A very similar theory of architecture was postulated a few years later by Le Corbusier in his *Vers une architecture*. He showed that plastic creation is 'dictated partly by the utilitarian demands of the problem, and partly by imagination' which stems from the plan—the static condition—and involves the masses and the surfaces which the architect works 'plastically'. The comparison of these two theories is in no way odious. In basic outline they are very similar, although Le Corbusier is thinking in terms of an architecture of primary forms brought together under a strict geometric discipline. Mendelsohn saw a danger of 'purely intellectual construction' with this approach.

When Le Corbusier speaks of form as 'the lineaments of the outward aspects', Mendelsohn would talk

*Luckenwalde Hat Factory for Steinberg–Herrmann. General layout*

*The dye-vat, Luckenwalde factory*

*Interior of a workshop, Luckenwalde factory*

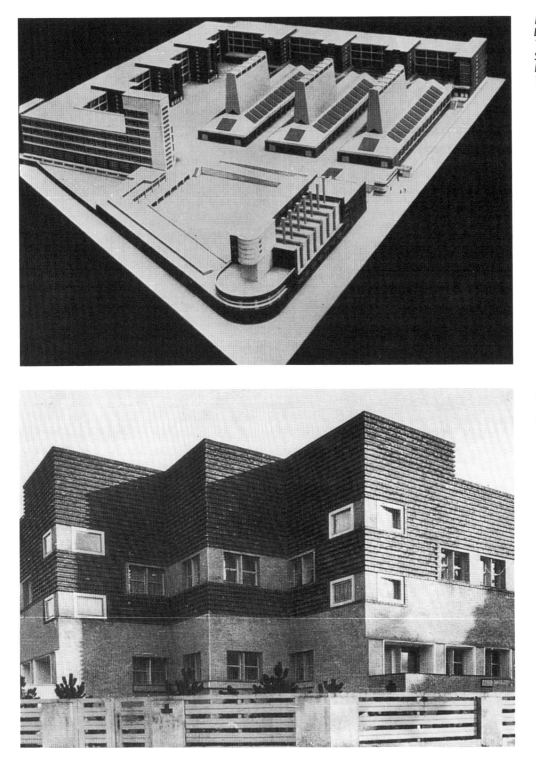

Factory for the
Leningrad Textile
Trust, 'Krasnoje
Snamja',
Leningrad, 1925.
View of model

Double villa,
Karolinger Square,
Berlin, Charlotten-
burg-West End,
1922

of the 'dynamic condition'. Probably the most important fact that comes out of this comparison is that their definition of architecture is so similar; Le Corbusier wrote:

'Architecture is the skilful, accurate and magnificent play of masses seen in light; and contours are also and exclusively the skilful accurate and magnificent play of volumes seen in light. Contours go beyond the scope of the practical man, the daring man, the ingenious man; they call for the plastic artist. . . . Architecture is the masterly, correct and magnificent play of masses brought together in light.'[15]

The grandiloquent phrasing of Mendelsohn's own idealism is reflected in his statement that 'Architecture is the only tangible expression of space of which the human spirit is capable'.[16] It bears repetition!

'Architectural beauty is not based on any representational forms which new constructions may borrow from history and self-complacently invent. Architectural beauty . . . must express in plan and appearance our own times' requirements and perceptions. The rediscovered union between function and appearance has freed architecture from scholarly isolation, and has connected it again to the life that is ours.'[17]

There is in Mendelsohn's architecture during the early years of the twenties a certain restlessness which can be best described in terms of empathy. As Adolf Behne wrote in his important book *Der moderne Zweckbau* in 1923:

'The desire for a more pronounced character and expressive individuality leads Mendelsohn in his Einstein Tower, and less markedly in his Mosse building (Berlin 1921–3) to an architecture that is deeply concerned with movement . . . which one can definitely describe as dramatic in van de Velde's sense and which is to be understood throughout within the movement of Expressionism. The entrance 'sucks', the walls 'lead', the staircase 'swings', etc.[18]

It is to van de Velde that Behne looks for influence for the Einstein Tower: 'Erich Mendelsohn's Einstein Tower at Potsdam shows amongst other things the powerful influence of van de Velde on the younger European architects.'[19] Mendelsohn in many of his writings indicated the enormous debt he owed to the Belgian architect. To Mendelsohn he was a 'father' figure.

Curt Behrendt is reported to have said in 1919 that the Einstein Tower was 'subjective . . . with too many remainders and ostentatious elements', a criticism that certainly could not be levelled at Mendelsohn's next major building, the hat factory for Steinberg, Herrmann and Company at Luckenwalde. Mendelsohn was engaged in the design and erection of this factory from 1921 to 1923 and the building is certainly one of the finest he ever built. The external forms of the buildings were not Expressionist in the same sense as the Einstein Tower was, although they still reflected something of the Expressionist *genre* in their sharp angularity. They can be compared to the splintered forms used by Lyonel Feininger in his woodcuts and sketches at that time.

The highly organized complex of buildings, all symmetrically planned, were constructed in reinforced concrete and brickwork, the use of which in angular and straight areas accentuated the unity of the scheme. The four great sheds and the dye-vat were constructed from portal frames, these were two storeys high and the openings between the smaller upper portals acted as lay lights to the buildings. The Dutch brickwork treatment of the exterior was stressed by the projection of alternate horizontal

courses. Mendelsohn re-used the forms of the dye-vat of the Luckenwalde factory in a scheme for a textile works at Leningrad in 1925, but there the shaped form of the large buildings were surrounded by an uninteresting four-storey L-shaped block.

Mendelsohn himself compared the Luckenwalde dye-works to the Public Baths at Hilversum with its expressive tower, demonstrating a certain sympathy with the work of the Dutch romantics. The dye-works, he said later, 'has a definite emotional element, and yet remains a purely utilitarian structure'.[20]

The Amsterdam architects, particularly the editor-in-chief of the magazine *Wendingen*, H. Th. Wijdeveld, first took an interest in Mendelsohn after notices on his sketches in the 'Architecture in Steel and Concrete' exhibition in 1919 had appeared in the press. Soon after this, he invited Mendelsohn to visit Holland and to lecture on architecture. Although he was greatly impressed by the architecture he saw, and although undoubtedly it was something of a turning-point in his career, Mendelsohn did not respond to the picturesque arts and crafts ideas of the Amsterdam architects as they had hoped he might. He quickly saw during his visit to Holland the dichotomy that existed between 'visionary Amsterdam' and 'analytical Rotterdam' and wrote to his wife:

'Oud is functional, corresponding to Gropius. Amsterdam is dynamic. Analytical Rotterdam refuses vision; visionary Amsterdam does not understand cold objectivity. Certainly the primary element is function; but function without sensibility remains mere construction. More than ever I stand by my reconciliatory programme. Both are necessary, and both must find each other. If Amsterdam goes a step further towards ratio, and Rotterdam's blood does not freeze, then they may unite. Otherwise,

Rotterdam will pursue the way of mere construction with deathly chill in its veins, and Amsterdam will be destroyed by the fire of its own dynamism. Function plus dynamics is the challenge.'[21]

When building work started in earnest again in Germany in 1924, after the inflationary period following the First World War, the commercial store became an important building type. Mendelsohn was commissioned to design a number of these very large buildings in major German towns—the Herpich Fur Store, Berlin, 1924, the Schocken Department Stores in Nuremberg and Stuttgart, the Petersdorff Store, Breslau during 1926–7 and the Schocken Store at Chemnitz in 1928–9.

With these shops at this very busy period of his life Mendelsohn created an 'image' for the modern store building that was to be copied and repeated almost at random throughout Western Europe. The repetitive motif of long horizontal bands of windows, that had originated in Hans Poelzig's office and shop building at Breslau in 1912, was again the most noticeable feature of the designs. In the powerful Stuttgart Schocken store the introduction of strong vertical emphases such as the staircase towers, and the use of enormous lettering on the main façade to contrast with the horizontality of the windows shows, as Aldous Huxley wrote in an article on 'aesthetic puritanism', that Mendelsohn was 'never afraid . . . of the fine, impressive, even spectacular gesture'.[22] Huxley goes on to talk of Mendelsohn's big shops in glowing terms; as grandiose, baroque buildings: 'with their bold alternation of planes and sweeping curves, their square or streamlined towers, their insistent striation—stripe above horizontal stripe—of iron and glass, (they) are as spectacular in their utterly different style as seventeenth-century churches.'[23]

In the sketches that continued to occupy his hand at this time Mendelsohn suggested in simple line form the general constructional principles as well as the finished appearance—still with uncanny skill and foresight—of the store buildings.

But of all the buildings in this, Mendelsohn's most creative period, it was the vast Universum Cinema (1926/9) that best demonstrated his skill as an architect. The building itself was a clean, crisp structure, its smooth façade curving gently around the corner of Berlin's fashionable Kurfürstendamm.

Mendelsohn's work by 1928 had become distinctly personal and his approach to architectural problems consistent and confident. He tackled domestic, entertainment, commercial and competition work with ease, and still found time for travel and writing. Although his buildings of this period had little to do with the visionary phase of the immediate postwar years, its effect on his sketching and thinking could still be detected. This can be seen in the drawings for the interior of the Universum and in a poem composed to commemorate its inauguration; an expressive piece of writing that gives a mental picture of his building, with its powerfully curved interior and its flat tortoise-shaped exterior, as clearly as one of his sketches.

It was pure Expressionist poesy, written in Mendelsohn's 'telegram' style:

'Cinema?

Pictures, theatre of motion!

Motion is life,

Real life is genuine, simple and true,

Therefore no affectation, no sentimentality.

Not in the pictures, not on the screen, not in building.

Show what it contains, what it is and what its own limitations are.

Theatre?—Not at all!

Elevator for the screen when the Sketch is succeeded by the film.—

Advertisement tower—Artificial architecture?—On the contrary!

Ventilation outlets (change of air, three times an hour) go straight out in the direction of the Kurfürstendamm:

For there we are: Universum—the whole world—the façades of a palace?—and the profitability: shops make money, offices vivify the scene and procure a public.

Porch entrance for high society?

Mouth opened widely and flooded with light, decorated in splendour.

For—you are to go in, everyone—into life, to the film, to the pay-box!

Cathedral cupolas? What for! Tortoise-shaped roof, projecting curves of the sloping ceiling, going towards the screen wall.

Ah! Camera!

Right!

Screen—the outside world.

Pictures—the bright life, tears, circus and moonlight at the sea-side.

We spectators—thousand, two thousand retinas, which suck up and reflect, each one happy or living an experience. Thus, no rococo-castle for Buster Keaton, no stucco pastries for Potemkin and Scapa Flow.

But, also, no fear!

No sober reality, no claustrophobia of life-weary brain acrobats—

Fantasy!

Fantasy—but no lunatic asylum—dominated by space, colour and light.

Under the swinging circle of the foyer, the street disappears, under the conical beams of the ceiling lights, the haze of evening disappears.

Then—left or right pass by the beacon of the pay-box into the twilight of the passage—Here you surely meet "them".

Bend down in tension!

Compressor!

But then full speed.

All planes, curves and light waves flash from the ceiling to the screen through the medium of music into the flickering image—into the Universe.'[24]

In May 1930 Mendelsohn expounded his theory of architecture in a lecture entitled 'Architecture of

The 'Universum' Cinema,
Berlin, 1926–9

Auditorium of the
'Universum'

*Peterdorff department store, Breslau, 1926–7*

our own Times', to the Architectural Association in London. It was a theory that had been forming since 1923 and that had by 1930 consolidated the twin poles of 'dynamics' and 'function'—the relation of the spiritual to the real. Or to put it into modern terms, a coupling of the emotional to the purposeful. 'Instead of Function put reality, conscience, reason . . . instead of Dynamic put unreality, feeling, imagination. It is perfectly clear', Mendelsohn said, 'that real creative power is the result of the interplay of dynamics and function.'[25]

By this time Mendelsohn was at the height of his career, having become the most successful architect of the *Berliner Kreis*. By this time too, he was able to see his work within the perspective of history, as a continuation of a tradition that displayed a concern with the three-dimensional possibilities of architectural form. He found, so he said in the lecture, that there was a certain affinity to his own thesis that architecture 'depends on the sensuous seizure by means of touch and sight' in a building such as the Palazzo Barbarano at Vicenza. Here, the wall had become 'an element of the structure', and he examined this particular example to demonstrate his concern for the three-dimensional possibilities of architecture. 'The difference between wall and front is a two-dimensional one. If we extend it further to the whole building, that is to say, if we consider it three-dimensionally, we get the contrast between space and surface.'[26]

It was here he suggested that the sensuous element becomes apparent, '. . . suggestive of space but no longer space pure and simple'. To make his point clearer in terms of contemporary architecture he said that Frank Lloyd Wright's Buffalo building 'shoots with tremendous energy into the air, catches the light, and thus gains shadow and depth. In a word it creates space. . . .'[27]

Mendelsohn had always spoken of architecture in terms of space and the effect of light and shadow on buildings, and in this lecture he castigated one of the villas at the *Werkbund's* Weissenhof Siedlung at Stuttgart, where the first collective manifestation of the *Neue Sachlichkeit* approach to architecture was to be seen in 1927, by stating that 'the architectonic super-structure is merely an expression of the ground plan. . . .'[28] One can see in his work of this time that the purely 'Functional' approach could never have been sufficiently spatial or expressive enough for him, because as he said much later, 'Function . . . as a mode of architectural action (was) dependent solely on conditions of use, material and construction'.[29] Architecture for Mendelsohn must be related to the 'dynamic condition', which contains 'an equilibrium of forces which, beyond its mechanical meaning, has a decisive symbolical significance'.[30]

By 1933 Mendelsohn was forced by expatriation to cut dead his success in Germany. Fleeing from the race and *Kultur*-hounding of the National Socialists, he arrived in England in that year, after visiting his 'venerated master' van de Velde in Belgium. He had a very mixed reception in this country; hostility from the more conservative architects and an open-arm welcome from those who admired his work. Of the latter, he quickly found he had a friend in Charles Reilly at Liverpool, who incidently referred to him as 'the most brilliant architect in Europe of the modern school'.[31] Within a few years Mendelsohn and his wife moved on to the United States, leaving the De La Warr Pavilion at Bexhill-on-Sea (won in competition together with his partner Serge Chermayeff in 1934) as a constant reminder of his short stay in this country.

Unfortunately, his work in America and later in Israel never assumes the power of his earlier work in Germany and in any reappraisal of his contribution to the development of modern architecture, particularly that of the expressionist-visionary type, must be given second place. In the Berlin period the influential buildings were the Einstein Tower, the Luckenwalde Hat Factory; the Schocken Stores at Nuremberg, Stuttgart and Chemnitz—with the emphasis on the horizontal band window; the fine Universum Cinema on the Berlin Kurfürstendamm and Columbus House. These buildings, together with a theory that 'architecture is the only tangible expression of space of which the human mind is capable' are the keys to the beginning of the creative work of a brilliant twentieth-century architect.

# 10

# Amsterdam and the Phantasts

The work of the Amsterdam school constitutes one of the first attempts in the twentieth century at a more plastic, freely decorated architecture. At first the efforts of the school were limited to little more than a rather self-conscious façadism. But under the hands of the masters of the school, Michel de Klerk (1884–1923) and Piet Kramer (born 1881), it became a conscious, spatially controlled architecture. The active life of this school of 'phantasts' was long in comparison to the short interval of postwar Expressionism in Germany. Its beginnings can be dated from 1913, the year in which van der Meij began the building of his major work, *Het Scheepvaarthuis* (the head offices of the Dutch Shipping Society), in the centre of Amsterdam. By the early twenties the school had reached its peak, only to die out rather rapidly—except for the work of a few, more conservative, members of the group—after de Klerk's untimely death in 1923 at the early age of thirty-nine, and after the success of the rival group, *de Stijl*, in international circles.

The *Scheepvaarthuis* represented a break with tradition; it was a formidable structure, constructed in reinforced concrete and clothed in a skin of terra-cotta and ornamental brickwork. Its appearance is almost beyond description. Although extravagantly overdecorated it marks an important change in the thinking of Dutch architects in that it was a distinct attempt to solve the duality of load-bearing and non-load-bearing elements; its decorative veneer belies the constructional logic behind the design. In the design of the building van der Meij was assisted by Michel de Klerk and Piet Kramer. After the erection of the *Scheepvaarthuis* and with some of their later housing projects these three architects experienced a lot of opposition from the general public as well as from informed architectural critics. As Mieras wrote, they 'incurred the odium of being virtuosos in the creation of architecture which was certainly brilliant but yet meaningless; architecture resplendent with excessive detail, arresting by its fantastic effect, but without any core'.[1]

Bearing in mind that in the *Scheepvaarthuis* the designers had set themselves a structural and expressive problem, and although it may appear today as a hybrid monster covered in trivial applied ornament, it does fit fairly comfortably between the Dutch *Art Nouveau* phase and the later more mature work of the same 'phantasts'. It was most certainly an extreme example of the way 'the flesh, not to say the fat, or *Art Nouveau*, had been grafted onto the dry bones of functionalism'.[2]

Of all the Continental currents in architecture, the Dutch flowed the smoothest; assimilating its influences from the rationalism of Berlage, the love for natural materials and good workmanship, and eventually the ideas of Frank Lloyd Wright. Holland was not undermined by war or internal rebellion and therefore its architectural development in the first three decades of this century was a more continuous one than that of Germany. Before the 1914–18 war had brought about a completely divided and disrupted Europe, Holland had only one major internal building problem, and that was the problem of overcrowding in its main cities. Therefore it was in Holland, much earlier than in Germany, that new schemes and ideas for mass tenement houses began, and it was largely due to the need for a rapid increase in housing that the new ideas for an architecture of elevations developed.

The government inspired housing programme began in earnest in the suburb of Amsterdam in the two years before the war. Here large areas of reclaimed land were allocated for row upon row of apartment houses. In this vast rehousing programme an 'Elizabeth Arden' type of face-lift technique was introduced, in which the architect was usually commissioned merely to add the beauty of his façade to the ingenuity of the builders' plan. Much of the freedom architects were given in their design of the façades, and in the 'extras' they felt a scheme needed, was due to the encouragement they received from the then Director of Housing in Amsterdam, Aerie Keppler.

Internally the planning of the housing left much to be desired and in no way coincided with the often marked originality of the exterior. The architects' fee for this kind of apron architecture, according to a popular rumour in Amsterdam, was remitted on the basis of so many guilders per lineal metre of the façade, regardless of vertical height! Of course not all the housing was done in this rather slapdash way. The work of architects like de Klerk, Kramer, Staal, Gratama, Rutgers and Wijdeveld, who often collaborated closely with contractors and housing societies, towers over the other run of the mill productions by its sheer imaginative skill, as well as in its use of ornament and brick, and the employment of well contrived architectural features. With the work of lesser architects the adaptation of plans to meet elevational needs and the provision of elaborate elevations that tried to cover up inconsistencies in planning was a basic weakness of the Amsterdam approach, a weakness that led many architects to indulge in the sin of over-detailing. It became for many too a style that, as R. Blijstra has said, 'was soon represented by a collection of stage scenery designed by smart people, behind which they hid their bad planning.'[3]

The small repetitive dwelling units in the housing schemes were often coordinated by horizontal bands of balconies and by large areas of brickwork, liberally peppered with decorative entrance loggias and ornamental turrets. These elements were scattered, at times it seems at random, over the façades of the long, malleable, horizontal projects.

The Amsterdam School consisted of a number of architects, craftsmen, artists and designers who came together with certain common principles; principles of workmanship, decoration and form. They all met

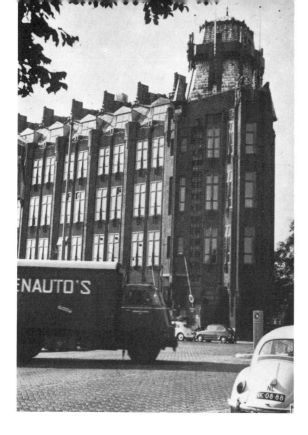

*J. M. van der Meij:* Het Scheepvaarthuis, Amsterdam

under the mutual contact of *Wendingen*, the magazine voice of a society known as *Architectura et Amicitia*. *Wendingen*—a title that implies something like 'turning point' in English—was edited by the architect H. Th. Wijdeveld. It acted as an enormous double-folded blotting paper absorbing traditional inspirational sources and influences from outside Holland after its first appearance in January 1918.[4] In its pages the work of contemporary Dutch architects, designers and graphic artists was featured side by side with work from abroad that appeared to be sympathetic towards Amsterdam and more particularly to Wijdeveld's own ideas. Special issues were devoted to the designs of the German Expressionist architects and special features appeared on rather monumental contemporary German buildings.

The magazine reflected to a certain extent the Expressionist tendencies of the German architects but it did not display, as Taut's magazine *Frühlicht* did, a passionate revolutionary zeal or a conviction of the need of a *Zukunftskathedrale*. No doubt this was because the Dutch were convinced that their role was to carry on and develop the more traditional ideas of the architects of the older generation; Cuijpers, de Bazel and the graphic artists Jan Toorop and Thorn-Prikker were admired by Wijdeveld just as much as Mendelsohn and Finsterlin. The unwritten thesis that can be discerned within the pages of *Wendingen* is that the work of the Amsterdam 'phantasts' was seen as the logical Dutch development of the *Art Nouveau-Jugendstil* phase.

The real roots of the magazine and those of its editor, Wijdeveld, were clearly in the work of Berlage and Frank Lloyd Wright. Throughout the publishing history of *Wendingen*, Berlage rests like an *éminence*

133

*grise* between its pages, while the treatment that Frank Lloyd Wright receives in special issues devoted to his work is one of selectivity and pointed analogy, Wijdeveld again seeming to say that the features he liked best about Wright's work are the ones that fit in with the Amsterdam school's attitude to architecture. Great prominence is therefore given in the photographs used in the magazine to those buildings of Wright's that bear a touch of fantasy and romanticism, such as the Midway Gardens at Chicago of 1913 and the Imperial Hotel at Tokyo of 1917. Later in the early 1920s, it has been said, that 'Wright's idiom became one of the chief ingredients of Dutch architectural expression'.[5]

Wright's actual introduction to the Dutch architectural world goes back much earlier than this, Wijdeveld himself claiming to have seen illustrations of his work in a book as early as 1900. Wijdeveld, who was then only fifteen, was so struck by what he saw, that he said 'I could not sleep the first night I possessed the book; I was so thrilled'.[6] In that same year of 1900 C. R. Ashbee, the English Arts and Crafts movement 'moralist', met Frank Lloyd Wright in Chicago, and began what was to prove to Europe to be an important friendship. In 1910 Ashbee was asked by the Berlin publisher Ernst Wasmuth to produce a monograph on Wright. This he did, bringing out also for the same publisher a few months later another edited version of Wright's work. This was called *Frank Lloyd Wright*; *Ausgeführte Bauten*, and appeared in 1911.

Through this publication Wright was successfully introduced to German circles, although it was not until after the war that any further volumes appeared in German on his work. Beyond the casual glance Wijdeveld claims to have had of Wright's work in 1900, it was left to Berlage and van 't Hoff to introduce Wright's architecture and ideas to Holland. During 1911–12 Berlage visited the United States; Robert van 't Hoff also went at about the same time. The effect of Wright's work on these two men was immediate—they had found a soul mate in a land as far away as the United States, who seemed to be interpreting in a twentieth-century way the tradition of Dutch brick architecture. Robert van 't Hoff almost literally brought Wright houses back in his luggage and introduced the low overhanging roofs, the carefully modulated reinforced concrete piers and the plan organization of Wright's designs—*ipso facto*—into his two villas at Huis ter Heide near Utrecht in 1916.

In Jan Wils's restaurant, *de Dubelle Sleutel* of 1919, a powerful Wrightian influence can also be distinguished, although there is in this scheme some argument as to whether the influence came directly from a knowledge of Wright's buildings or via the evangelizing activity of van 't Hoff and Berlage.[7]

Besides the concern to promote Wrightian principles of architecture to *Wendingen*'s select public, Wijdeveld and the Amsterdam group also had many other interests—interests that ranged from Oriental and Eastern art to anthropology and geology. Wider international aspects, reflecting the admiration Wijdeveld held for the visionary architects, are to be seen in the publication of articles and special editions on Josef Hoffmann, Erich Mendelsohn (it is in this issue on Mendelsohn that Oskar Beyer

*The pepper-pot balcony and bay treatment typical of the work of the architects of the 'Amsterdam School'*

135

refers to Mendelsohn as an 'Expressionist' architect), Hermann Finsterlin, Hans Poelzig, as well as on the enchanting work of the Viennese graphic artist, Gustav Klimt.[8]

Michel de Klerk was the most original and the most important architect of the Amsterdam school.[9] His work was less inhibited than the work of his contemporaries (with the possible exclusion of his friend Piet Kramer), yet it always achieved a fine sense of order. The housing scheme designed by de Klerk in 1913 for the housing organization *Eigen Haard*, around the Spaarndammerplantsoen in Amsterdam West, is the first example of his carefully controlled and essentially human approach. With its careful use of spatial elements and emphasis on brickwork features it was a premonition of the work he was to do for the same organization on another estate facing the Zaanstraat, a few yards away, four years later. Here in his best-known work he designed more or less a complete community under one roof. On an almost triangular site he grouped a post office, community buildings and tenements in a closely compacted peripheral scheme; to which, at a later date, a cunningly devised secondary school was added. This scheme was more than a mere façadism, the internal spaces being as valid architecturally as the external features, which show a marked originality, even for de Klerk. A vertical tile-hung feature shaped like a thin church spire was carefully positioned on the base of the triangular site so that it is seen from both Hembrugstraat—which is recessed back at this point—and the internal courtyards. The main five-storey block of tenements stretches along the sides of the triangle, along Oostzaanstraat and Zaanstraat itself; while at the apex end of the site, the prow-like projection of the bay windows above the post office brings the development down to two storeys again. All the horizontal elements in the scheme, balconies, string courses and the consistent positioning of the ground floor windows give it a basic unity. The workmanship both of the brickwork and the tile hanging is of the highest quality; the subtleties of the brickwork treatment itself having been worked out in many cases on the site during the course of the building's erection.

De Klerk's lineage is as strange as his architecture; born in Amsterdam on 24 November 1884, he was the twenty-fifth son of a seventy-five year old father. His training in architecture had been in the *atelier* of Edward Cuijpers, where he stayed for fourteen years. It was here that his profitable friendship began with two fellow pupils, J. M. van der Meij and Piet Kramer.

De Klerk was not only a highly imaginative architect and a fine draughtsman but also an accomplished watercolourist and furniture designer. His portrait drawings of such sitters as Cuijpers and Toorop indicate a remarkable sensitivity.[10] His early architectural projects, many of which were competition entries submitted under various pseudonyms, have a confident exploratory touch and a freedom from eclecticism, although they still seem to lack any real connection with the pioneer modern work going on in other countries at that time. Indeed as Staal said in an article in *Wendingen* on the early projects, 'de Klerk was niet modern'.[11]

What de Klerk was exploring was a world of precise architectural detailing and applied decoration, attempting as he went along to make an architecture of quality and taste. In this his attitude was almost Ruskinian. Ruskin had said that 'Ornamentation is the principal part of architecture', an equivocal law

*Michel de Klerk: the* Eigen Haard *housing development, Amsterdam, 1921*

*The* Eigen Haard *housing from the* Zaanstraat

137

*Housing along the Zaanstraat, window detail*

*Michel de Klerk: housing on the Henrietta Ronnerplein, Amsterdam*

perhaps, but a law to which de Klerk paid more than lip-service.[12] Ruskin, in his *Lectures on architecture and painting*, praised the street architecture of the Netherlands and the Low Countries for the fantasy and variety to be found in its ornamentation; as well as for its 'endless perspective'. 'In the Netherlands and Northern France,' he wrote, 'where the material for building is brick and stone, the fronts of the stone gables are raised above the roofs and you have magnificent and grotesque ranges of steps or curves decorated with various ornaments.'[13]

It is precisely within such a tradition that de Klerk worked. He was a true romantic, steeped in the culture of his own country, having a self-appointed task of reinterpretation. This can be further demonstrated by examining the houses he designed on the Henriette Ronnerplein of 1921, where he linked together a series of completely separate houses (derived from his earlier *dubbel* house designs of 1915) by their extended gable ends, to form a piece of street architecture; each unit thus became a part of a continuous façade. The division between each unit was further accentuated by a tall chimney and a sunken, circular flowerbox at each break, thus giving the scheme paradoxically a unity in diversity.

After de Klerk, Piet Kramer was the most significant and successful member of the Amsterdam school. Many of his buildings, which are also still situated in the suburbs of Amsterdam, have a less aggressive nature than those of de Klerk; they are more feminine, a contrast to de Klerk's masculinity. The

*Piet Kramer:* De Dageraad *housing development, Amsterdam*

Below: *Detail of the tower and turret detail, in the* De Dageraad *housing scheme*

J. F. Staal: model of office building, Amsterdam

flowing curves of brickwork in the houses he built for the *De Dageraad* housing association, on the P. L. Takstraat in 1921–23 (designed in 1918), smoothly turn the corners of the block to join the long straight runs of plain brick façade. Architectural emphasis is given here by raising the corners of the blocks so that they stand out like fortresses from the main straight façade.

P. L. Kramer, who was three years older than de Klerk, set up practice on his own account in 1913 after completing the work on the *Scheepvaarthuis* with van der Meij and de Klerk. His own work was less flamboyant than the *Scheepvaarthuis* and much less bizarre and original than some of de Klerk's designs. The Sailors' Federation Building in Den Helder was his first major project. Built during 1914–16 it was a simple brick structure possessing a bulky, towerlike appearance which from some angles looked like a respectable, late Georgian, English parsonage. Only the top of the tower itself and the ornamental walls around the terrace indicate any leanings towards the decorative exuberance of some of his later designs. In his designs for tenements and private houses the lingering influence of seventeenth- and eighteenth-century traditionalism can be detected; an influence that was linked to a knowledge of and an admiration for English domestic building at the turn of the century. Wijdeveld in describing Kramer's four houses in the Park Meerwijk at Bergen, built in 1916–17, said they possessed 'the atmosphere that Norman Shaw knew well', and that they bore a very close resemblance to the work of Lutyens, Baillie Scott and Voysey. At Bergen the Park Meerwijk layout was a notable example of the extreme romantic tendencies of the Amsterdam school of architects.[14] Here such architects as Kramer, Blaauw, Staal and La Croix together carried out, as one writer has said, an 'exceptional architectural experiment'.[15] While, as Wijdeveld wrote in *Wendingen*, 'Amid these individualistic and expressionistic architects came also the work of our first Dutch woman architect, Margaret Kropholler'.[16]

J. M. Luthmann:
*Radio Station,
Kootwijk, near
Apeldoorn, 1922*

It is to Margaret Kropholler that one must look to find the strangest creations in the Park. She designed one of the houses, *Huize Beukenhoek*, to resemble a boat, the body of the house being thatched over and the terrace surrounded by a wall shaped like a ship's prow. This is a veritable Noah's Ark; although, incidently, it is Staal's house in the Park that is called *Huize de Ark*. If the urban work of the school had emphasized the quality of malleable brickwork, it was in the country, with small domestic properties, that the emphasis was on the rural industries of thatching and wrought timber.

The Dutch emphasis on eccentricity of form and on traditional craftsmanship was taken a stage further in the work of the two partnerships, Eibink and Snellebrand and Vorkink and Wormser. In an article on the work of the firm of Vorkink and Wormser in *Wendingen*, the very ship-shaped country houses built at Oostvoorne are illustrated which show the way, through sketches and a model, these architects attempted to use straw thatching plastically, cutting and cropping the thatch as if it were a flexible, workable material like reinforced concrete. The freely shaped plans of these houses reflect some of the utopian ideas submitted to the *Arbeitsrat für Kunst* exhibition in Berlin for 'Unknown Architects' in 1919.

142

In absorbing contemporary ideas from outside the Netherlands the most obvious connections, apart from those already mentioned between the Berlin *avant-garde* and *Wendingen*, are those with the German Monumentalists. J. Luthmann in his group of buildings designed for the Radio Station at Kootwijk, near Apeldoorn, which were opened in 1922, attempted a monumental symbolism. Set in the barren heathlands of central Holland the crisp geometry of the layout and the moulded forms of the main building's reinforced concrete structure is much nearer to the classicism inherent in German monumental architecture than to the picturesqueness of Luthmann's fellow Amsterdam School architects; nearer that is, to the monumental aspects of Behrens's work for AEG in Berlin and to the buildings of Poelzig, Berg and Paul Bonatz.

Dutch architectural fantasy on the whole was quite different from the German, it was less emotional, and generally Dutch architects were not committed to any particular synthesis of architecture and the arts, or for that matter concerned with the creation of a Utopian society. Monumentalism too was an isolated episode. Wijdeveld certainly had the intention of courting the approval of architects such as Mendelsohn, Poelzig and Finsterlin for the extravagances of the Amsterdam school's work, however, if there was any reciprocation of ideas it was only recalled in the occasional employment of Dutch brickwork treatment in some of Mendelsohn's buildings and in the work of the more conservative German Expressionist architects, Hoetger, Höger and Kreis.

The admiration of the visionary architects in the various Berlin groups was directed to the other more powerful and internationally orientated *de Stijl* group which originated in Leiden in 1917. The concern for rationalism and the attempted marriage of form and function, displayed in the *Stijl* group's work, was a direct contrast to the whimsy of the Amsterdam approach.

# 11

Buildings will begin to speak. They will speak a
language of which men at the present have
no inkling  *Rudolf Steiner* 1914

# Rudolf Steiner and the way to
# a new style in architecture

An analysis of the architecture of Expressionism, particularly in its most self-conscious and enigmatic phase, would not be complete without reference to the work of Rudolf Steiner.

Although Steiner's architectural ideas and so-called 'aesthetic laws' were developed before the time of the exaggerated and vigorous postwar ideas of the Berlin circle, his completed buildings were an important contribution to the romantic stream within the Modern Movement. In time, Steiner's work is contemporary with that of the Amsterdam 'phantasts', but totally different in spirit.

Rudolf Steiner (1861–1925), philosopher, Goethe scholar and occultist, was not a trained architect. But he did design buildings, discourse on the merits of a new style in architecture, and gather around himself craftsmen and artists to interpret his own ideas on the way architecture should develop. In many ways he was a modern *Uomo Universale*, around whom all disciplines are brought together as part of a way of life. Like the Renaissance masters he awarded architecture the pride of first place among the arts. He brought to the study of architecture and aesthetics a knowledge of mathematics, history and literature, as well as an experimental knowledge of philosophy and science. It is impossible to divorce Steiner's views on architecture from his attitude to other aspects of life. This makes the study of his aesthetic views even more difficult to understand because as a philosopher he was free to invent his own vocabulary and symbolic ideas. In order to gain a deeper insight into Steiner's contribution to architecture it is necessary to examine briefly some of the details of his life. He was born an Austrian in Kraljevic in 1861; in the midst of a period that displayed an intense interest in applied science and new ways of life. His childhood was spent near Vienna, where at a very early age he became interested in classical languages and in mathematics. After leaving the Grammar school at Neustadt he entered the Technical University at Vienna to study science and mathematics. By 1883 and while still studying, he was invited to edit Goethe's scientific works for the well known Kürschner *National Literatur*. These writings, largely observations made by Goethe of natural phenomena and the so-called principles of creation, allowed Steiner to develop his own thoughts on the spiritual nature of science. Steiner shared with Goethe an awareness of the physical and spiritual duality in nature, a duality which in Steiner's view extended into mathematics and aesthetics. It was to the exposition of this problem that he devoted much of his life. On the ambivalence of mathematics and art he once wrote: 'As a child, I felt, though naturally I could not say it quite clearly: one must be able to carry in oneself knowledge of the spiritual world in the same way as one knows geometry.' He found 'in geometry a kind of knowledge apparently produced by man, but with a quite independent validity'.[1]

During his years at the *Realschule* Steiner enthusiastically pursued his interest in geometrical design and he says in his autobiography that 'the drawing of circles, lines and triangles' became his favourite occupation. He was constantly being driven to nature for inspiration, attempting to assimilate its laws in terms of mathematics, physics and geometry.

In 1888 Steiner was invited to Germany to help with the preparation of the Weimar edition of Goethe's works. After a short stay in Weimar, during which time he says he saw very little of its artistic life, he visited Berlin and Munich. In those cities his short visits were 'given over entirely to absorption in the art these places afforded'. On his return to Vienna he soon moved into the group of architects, *littérateurs* and artists who were meeting in the home of the theosophist Marie Lang.

Steiner's sociability was an important aspect of his life, and throughout Europe he came into contact with the intellectual and artistic *élite*. After moving back for a lengthy period into the cultural circle of Weimar he became acquainted with the protagonists of the 'modern conception' and intimately involved in the setting up of the Nietzsche Archive. He began to see Nietzsche as the complement of Goethe and took upon himself the role of middleman interpreting Goethe's sense of the spiritual reality of nature on the one hand and Nietzsche's vision of a spiritual mythology on the other.

In the years just before the turn of the century Steiner was attracted into the artistic and cultural circles of Berlin, and became acquainted with both Frank Wedekind and Paul Scheerbart. Steiner was immediately drawn to the unusual 'basic quality of soul in Paul Scheerbart', and although he found his poems grotesque and fantastic he felt the poet himself to be 'entirely lovable'. Steiner wrote in his autobiography about Scheerbart's work:

. . . one finds that a fantastic sense for all sorts of generally unobserved meanings in words derived from a fantasy of soul, not only without foundation, but not in the least seeking for a foundation. In Paul Scheerbart there was a vital inner cult of the fantastic, but one that moved in the sought-out forms of the grotesque.'[2]

While in Berlin and involved in the pre-Expressionist circles Steiner consolidated his own ideas into what he termed a 'spiritual science'. In 1902, at the age of forty-one, he became the leader of the German section of the Theosophical Society. Later he and his followers gradually broke away from that movement to form provisionally, in 1912, the first Anthroposophical Society. This movement of Anthroposophy took its name from the literal derivation of the Greek words, *Anthropos*—man, *Sophos* —wise, the wisdom of mankind. Man was placed in this concept, at the centre of all perceptions:

146

'Anthroposophy,' Steiner wrote in 1925, 'is the path of knowledge to guide the Spiritual in the human being to the Spiritual in the Universe. It arises as a need of the heart, of the life of feeling: and it can only be justified inasmuch as it can satisfy this inner need.'[3]

Anthroposophy was an occult sect, based largely on Christian teaching. It was typical of the many strong, pseudo-religious sects prevalent in the German atmosphere of Expressionism. Undoubtedly, it has been far more successful than its many, now extinct, sister cults. This is mainly because Steiner was himself a powerful and unique individual. In some ways he was akin—although never one himself—to the Expressionists; he embodied their zeal and revolutionary spirit in a deeply spiritual way. Almost apostolically he sought to create a new order, relating man and the world to a perception of rhythms of time. As Kenneth Bayes puts it, 'Rhythms which extend from the heart beat of man to the eons of great cosmic epochs'.[4]

This mystical approach extended into the world of Steiner's architecture. Indeed it was common to find that many of the other artists and architects involved in the search for new styles in art, life and architecture in the early part of this century, had an intense interest in similar but not so easily defined problems. H. L. C. Jaffé in his book on the Dutch de Stijl group of artists, indicates the interest of the members of that group in Theosophy.[5] While Alma Maria Werfel, in her rather perverse autobiography, mentions it with relation to the teachers at the Bauhaus.[6]

Steiner was a spiritual romantic who was inspired by the sensuous forms to be found in nature. In using these forms he appointed some a symbolic purpose and lent to others a static quality. Many of the forms he used and invented had a powerful erotic quality (or perhaps were unconscious fertility symbols), indicating, no doubt, his sympathy with nature. A similar tendency towards this kind of eroticism in art forms can be clearly seen in the religious and symbolic sculptures of primitive societies, and significantly Steiner talks at length in his lecture of 1914 to which he gave the title 'True Aesthetic Laws of Form', of the 'atavistic clairvoyance' that was an attribute of primitive man. 'Many of the forms to be found in primitive art can only be understood when we realize that they were the outcome of this primordial clairvoyant consciousness.'[7] By adapting these forms to his own philosophy Steiner was trying to imply the eternal validity of such forms.

Steiner's excursion into architecture began almost by accident, and quite late in his career. He had decorated a number of columns of an interior for a convention in Frankfurt and was approached by two mathematician/engineers about his seriousness as a designer and architect. This eventually led him to take his ideas further with a design for a temple type structure for a site in Munich. However, his application to erect the structure was later turned down by the Kaiser himself, as the site was opposite a well-known church and the law as it existed did not allow two religious buildings in close proximity. With his regard for, and background knowledge of, Goethe's work it seemed only appropriate that the main centre of the newly founded society should be named the 'Goetheanum'. This centre, 'a free high school for spiritual science', was finally established at Dornach, near Basel, in Switzerland. This was in 1913 and the building then erected, Goetheanum I, demands examination in detail as this was Steiner's major architectural work. The second Goetheanum, built to replace the first which was destroyed by fire on New Year's Eve, 1922–3, was opened in 1928, three years after Steiner's death. It remains incomplete.

Kenneth Bayes, an English architect recently responsible for a few buildings in the Steiner style, has also made an extensive study of the theoretical background to Steiner's architectural work.[8] Bayes is a prominent member of the Anthroposophical Society and is well acquainted with Steiner's writings. In an analysis of Steiner's architecture, which might be called 'architecture of the soul', Bayes has suggested that its three most important characteristics are:

1. Movement (particularly of line).
2. Sculptural form.
3. Metamorphosis of form.

It is the first quality of a restless kind of movement that is evident in the designs of Steiner at Dornach, a characteristic of so much of the romantically orientated buildings of the modern movement. This was also an essential characteristic of the continuing tradition that goes back to the buildings and furniture of the *Art Nouveau*, with their sinewy, sensuous, flamboyant forms. 'Steiner,' Bayes says, 'stressed the necessity in many spheres of activity . . . to bring into movement what had earlier been static. To become mobile and flexible.'[9] In stressing this moving, living quality of form, Steiner rephrased the linear qualities of the *Art Nouveau*; although he certainly denied the naturalistic elements inherent in the decorative style of that Movement. In his work, he came very near to Henri van de Velde's opinion of form and ornament, that 'the relation between . . . structural and dynamographic ornament and the form of the surfaces, should appear so intimate that the ornament seems to have determined the form.'[10]

The first Goetheanum suggests an affinity both to the work of van de Velde and to that of the Vienna Sezession; the craftsmanship is hand-in-glove with the flowing movement and outward form of the decoration. But these inferences remain only slight, as Steiner commanded a form language peculiarly his own. He married his sense of movement to the second characteristic of sculptural form, so that the buildings are moulded *en masse* and made to appear almost pliable. This can be seen more clearly in the house Steiner designed for himself and in the second Goetheanum, where the maquette for the project, made by Steiner out of Harbutt's red plasticine, is in the form of a jelly mould. This sculptural quality, and indeed the whole architecture of man was, for Steiner, 'the result of the interplay of earthly and cosmic forces'. Steiner's metaphysical ideas permeated this architecture of the soul. 'Architecture stands on the earth in a central position. ''A spiritual being'' on one hand, inspiring mankind; on the other a solid structure of brick or concrete serving a sensible earthly purpose.'[11]

Metamorphosis of form is the characteristic, culled from the writings and lectures, that is most commonly associated with Steiner's sculptural and architectural work. It is intrinsically bound up with the other characteristics of movement and sculptural form, although a distinctive notion in itself. It is an extremely difficult idea to define. Bayes suggests the following definition:

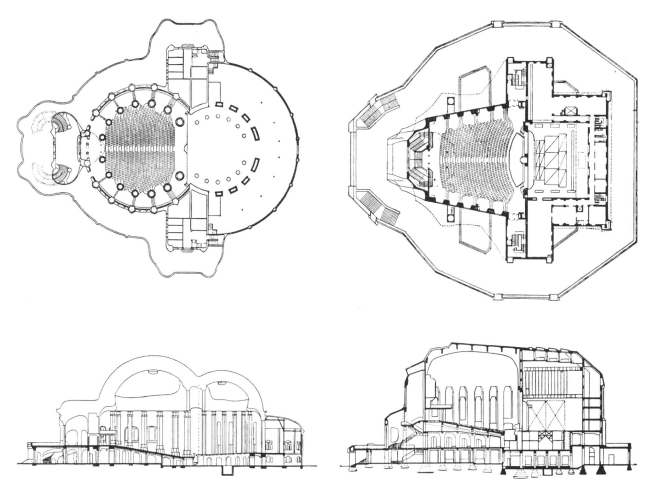

*Plans and longitudinal sections, Goetheanum I and Goetheanum II*

'Metamorphosis in terms of building means the repetition of a particular motif (or motifs) in different parts of the building. This must not be an exact repetition, but with the motif changed or developed in its form. The motif must not just be changed in any way, but changed in an organic development.'

This concept of metamorphosis is Steiner's unique contribution to modern architecture. Its origins are in the analysis Goethe made of the plant as an 'earthly image of a spiritual archetype. Budding and sprouting, the archetype being of the plant embodies itself through successive metamorphoses of form until it reaches its full expression.'

In seeking an elaboration of Goethe's ideas on metamorphosis Steiner attempted to express the relation between what he termed the 'living ideal forms through which the organic can be understood', and the 'formless ideas suited to enable one to grasp the inorganic'. Explaining these ideas in detail Steiner wrote:

149

'In understanding the inorganic, concept is added in series to concept, in order to survey the correlation of forces which bring about an effect in nature. In reference to the inorganic it is necessary so to allow one concept to grow out of another that in the progressive living metamorphosis of concepts there come to light images of that which appears in nature as a being possessing form.'

It does seem, however, that it is on this very issue of metamorphosis of form that Steiner's thesis, at least as he later relates it to architecture, is at its weakest. He seems to have extended the theory of empathy (*Einfühlung*)—the projection of bodily feelings into the forms of architecture—to give buildings themselves almost a natural life of their own. Metamorphosis by definition suggests a natural change, a transformation that has occurred by an inner, natural action, and as such is a type of change that cannot ever take place in an art so rigid as architecture. Steiner was in fact trying to create an environment in which the sum of the smaller, unrelated parts of a building would add up to a common, harmonious whole 'image', an idea common to the postwar Expressionist architects in Germany (i.e. Häring's idea of *Gestalt-werk*).

Steiner has an even closer connection with the Berlin Utopians in that his notion, that a building should be a living organism, comes very close to the ideas propounded by Hermann Finsterlin in his numerous drawings and articles on architectural form. But whereas Finsterlin presented an architecture in which the spaces themselves, the glands, had an organic validity, Steiner saw this organic quality in the surface area and structure of each building. 'The wall is not merely wall, it is living, just like a living organism that allows elevations and depressions to grow out of itself.'[12] Out of these walls the details of the building grow with a life of their own, as part of one organism: ' . . . inside our building we shall find *one* plastic form, a continuous relief sculpture on the capitals, plinths, architraves. They grow out of the wall, and the wall is their basis, their soil, without which they could not exist.'[13]

Undoubtedly with the first Goetheanum, he achieved his aim. The site for the building was on a ridge of one of the smaller foothills of the Jura mountain range, overlooking the city of Basel. Its outward shape was a strong contrast to the undulating countryside. During the period the building was being constructed, Steiner spoke of the new style in architecture saying that the present task was 'to translate the static, geometric structure of previous architectural forms into an organic dynamic method of designing and shaping'.[14]

At this time, 1913, he offered a philosophy and a building that was idiosyncratic and original. The building itself was comparable only in size and concept in Europe to the Centenary Hall built by Max Berg at Breslau in the same year. Goetheanum I was constructed entirely of timber resting on a huge reinforced concrete substructure. An enormous structure, it had a length of 272 feet, a width of 243 feet and a height, to the top of the largest of the two domes, of 111 feet. The plan was axial, running east–west, the building itself consisting of two circular spaces (cf. Gropius's Total Theatre) with an

*Goetheanum I under construction:* Above left: *February 1914.*
Left: *The roofing-in ceremony, April 1914*

*The shingle roofs of Goetheanum I*

auditorium and a stage fused together at the line of proscenium opening. The two main spaces were enclosed by the ingeniously constructed timber framed double-dome and surfaced with scolloped shingle tiles. The main area was then joined to three smaller hooded roofs covering the ancillary accommodation and the entrance hall. These roofs bore an uncanny resemblance to German military headgear.

Internally the auditorium was a riot of sensuous line, carved by hand from rough timbers. Each column—and there were fourteen altogether in the auditorium—was from a different wood. The capitals to these columns were carved 'into' rather than 'out from' the wood giving a tremendous sense of the asymmetric plasticity of form. 'Just as the interior decoration had the quality of being "in-carved",' Steiner said, 'so the outer decoration will seem as though it is "laid on".' He stressed that the essential thing is a 'true feeling for form in space'.[15]

Steiner's architecture is really open sculpture; huge pieces of sculpture in which people move and have a new sense of being. This is what he intended. It is not sculptural building in the sense that Mendelsohn or Le Corbusier referred to in their equation of architecture with the magnificent play of light on form. It is rather an environment above and around which the primary spaces are created to invoke the response of the Spirit in man. With Steiner the interior was all important. Whether the spaces he

*The timber constructed Goetheanum I on its reinforced concrete base*

153

actually created internally are totally satisfactory as 'architectural spaces' is another question. For him they were 'soul spaces' in which there was an important distinction between *real space*, which remains external to man, and *soul space* in which spiritual events, interior to man, were realized. In one of his lectures given during the building of the first Goetheanum at Dornach in 1914, Steiner drew an unusual but enlightening analogy between the internal and external spaces of the building:

'When we are trying to understand what will be placed in the interior of the building in these two different sized spaces (the domed spaces) we may with advantage think of the principle of the mould in which German cakes are baked. The cake rises in the mould and when it is taken out its surface shows all the forms which appear on the sides of the mould in negative. . . . All that is to be enclosed within the forms, all that is to be spoken and proclaimed, must be in correspondence, as the dough of the cake corresponds to the negative forms of the baking mould.'[16]

A study of Steiner's contribution to the architecture of Expressionism would not be complete without reference to his concern for colour, and colour symbolism. This is a concern that has been related in an earlier chapter with the work of the Expressionist painters. Steiner spoke of 'the creative world of colour'. He calls colour 'a living experience' relating it to an 'inner life-force'. 'It must be possible for us not merely to look at colours, to reproduce them outwardly here and there, but to live with colour, to experience the inner life-force of colour.'[17] Steiner's views on colour of course stem directly from Goethe; but they are ideas that were, as Michael Wilson has pointed out in his chapter in the book of essays commemorating the centenary of Steiner's birth, only *implied* in Goethe's own work. It was Steiner's aim that Goethe's own views should become *explicit*. Of Goethe's conception of colour Wilson writes:

'. . . his main idea was that colour arises as a result of the interaction of light and darkness, and that the principle of opposites (complementarity) is a fundamental feature of all colour experience. Another conviction was that the eye is created out of the forces of light, and therefore must contain the principles of light and colour within itself.'[18]

Steiner laid considerable stress on these ideas in his own theoretical writing on colour. And even though modern physicists have largely rejected such ideas, as Wilson points out, they have proved to be of considerable practical value. Even colourists of the calibre of Turner found in Goethe's *Farbenlehrer* a genuine source of inspiration.

Turner, like Goethe, found that colour evoked certain moods. This view was further elaborated by such protogenic Expressionists as Matisse and Gauguin.[19] Matisse said, to give but one example of this kind of approach to colour:

'To paint an autumn landscape I will not try to remember what colours suit this season, I will be inspired only by the sensation that the season gives me; the icy clearness of the sour blue sky will express the season just as well as the tonalities of the leaves. My sensation itself may vary, the autumn may be soft and warm like a protracted summer or quite cool with a cold sky and lemon yellow trees that give a chilly impression and announce winter.'[20]

*Goetheanum II, Rudolf Steiner's original model of the exterior*

*Goetheanum II, built to Steiner's original plans and built to last*

155

But to return to Steiner, in one of his lectures he goes on to find in colour—as he finds in the metamorphosis of form—a living, moving quality.

'It is impossible,' he said, 'to live into the essence of colour if one cannot immediately pass over from repose into movement, realizing that a red disc approaches us, and that a blue disc, on the other hand, withdraws. . . . The relation between the red that is painted on a figure, in contrast to the blue, is such that the figure takes on life and movement through the very colour itself.'[21]

He continues, with an analysis of the effect of form on colour.

'Form is of course the element that is at rest, stationary; but the moment the form has colour, the inner movement in the colour rises out of the form, and the whirl of the cosmos, the whirl of spirituality passes through the form . . . the colour you give to a particular form places this form into the whole concatenation of its environment and indeed the whole universe. . . . We breathe soul into dead form when, through colour, we make it *living*'.[22]

Whatever one may think of Steiner's metaphysics it must be remembered that it was with the very idea of the 'soul content' of colour and form that he produced the first and second Goetheanum buildings. In the stained glass windows of the first Temple of Spiritual Science the colour polarities of blue and red were to be seen as part of the drama of the building; as clearly an 'intimation of ineffable truth' as that propounded by Thierry and the school of Chartres in their great cathedral of Notre Dame.

Within ten years of its erection the first vast Temple of Spiritual Science was reduced to ashes. Almost immediately out of the conflagration arose a new and even more dynamic structure, Goetheanum II (begun in 1925), known affectionately to the adherents of Steiner's movement as The Building. This time it was more firmly constructed in reinforced concrete. Chronologically the two buildings indicate Steiner's progress as an architect. The experimental nature of the first building and the almost blind groping for the expression of new aesthetic laws gave way to the imposing sculptural mass of the second. However, Steiner only laid the foundation of this work. He died in 1925 at the age of sixty-four, three years before the building was officially opened, but not before he had given the general direction he wanted the building to take with a set of working drawings, a number of sketches and the 1/100th scale plasticine model of the exterior. These were all faithfully followed by his collaborators in the construction of the building, even though little indication had been given of the form the interior should take, or the pattern of the fenestration. The work on Goetheanum II was carried out under the direction of Ernst Aisenpreis and a team of artists and engineers. The chief structural engineer was a Norwegian, Olé-Falk Ebbell, who had worked with Steiner on the first building, and who had also been responsible for the erection of some of the minor buildings at Dornach that still stand in the vicinity of the second Goetheanum. These include the Gaudíesque boiler house (designed by Ebbell, 1915), the timber and glass constructed studio (1915), the odd-shaped transformer house, and a number of extremely bulky Expressionistic houses. It is these buildings particularly that give likely clues to the influences behind Steiner's work although no influences from *Art Nouveau*, the Weimar and Berlin circles, van de Velde or Gaudí will be allowed by any of his followers.

156

*Goetheanum II*

*Goetheanum II: details*

Boiler house, Dornach, 1913

The stained glass studios, Dornach, 1913

Haus Duldeck, 1913. This villa in the
grounds of the Goetheanum is now
used as a publishing house

Roof detail, Haus Duldeck

Goetheanum II, at present unfinished, appears to lack the subtlety of the fusion of interior spaces that was to be found in the first building. Its present strength lies in its compactness and in its powerful sculptural shape. Like the little church of Notre Dame du Haut, less than fifty miles away at Ronchamps, designed by Le Corbusier between 1950 and 1955, it is a piece of living sculpture. In many ways it is a building of the same character as Mendelsohn's Einstein Tower. Its external shape is bold and unusual, a powerful monolithic structure that has a compelling sense of external unity. Only the eccentric detailing of the windows—each of which is shaped differently, some are cut back halfway across the head, others tapered at the sides—betrays the rather self-conscious attempt to make it an 'original' building, otherwise it fits into its environment as a sculptural centrepiece. The concrete is left untreated, inside and out, the surface texture of the external face of the building having been made by the marks of the rough timber shuttering—another characteristic that is found in much of Le Corbusier's postwar work. Viewing this building objectively, it seems strange that modern architects have ignored it for so long, particularly since the revival of interest in the work of Gaudí in the early 1950s produced so much enthusiasm for this kind of plasticity of form and sculptural monolithy. No doubt a reappraisal of Steiner's contribution to the architecture of Expressionism—and it only just bursts the seams of the date limits given to this phase, 1910–23—in this post-Ronchamp era is valid, even if its connections with that Master from La Chaux-de-Fonds, which is just down the road from Dornach, are continuously denied. The connections are denied in the face of good evidence, for it was Le Corbusier himself who was speechless (according to Ebbell) when he visited the unfinished shell of the vast 'House of Speech', as Steiner liked to call his project, in 1926–7. Ebbell, when recalling the visit, is reported to have added: 'Someone like that doesn't forget an experience of that sort so soon; it sinks in. I am convinced that he carried it around with him for decades and that it emerged in his chapel.'

*Kenneth Bayes: classroom block at Peredur Home-school, East Grinstead. Main entrance*

*Le Corbusier: Notre Dame du Haut, Ronchamp, 1950–4*

165

**12**

# Conclusion: the aesthetics of Expressionist architecture

From the writings and buildings of the Utopian architects some idea of an Expressionist aesthetic can be deduced. There were of course, in this essentially individualistic and visionary period, no formal laws and no clear aesthetic doctrine, although from an examination of various projects a number of common aims and ideas can be found. This is consistent with the exploratory basis of Expressionism. In this concluding chapter I am introducing a rather personal analysis of the aesthetic basis of the architecture of the period in which the connection between the ideas of the architects and the general movement of international Expressionism will, I feel, become apparent.

Principally, the architects of the visionary phase sought a complete freedom of expression. They yearned for a Utopia in which revolutionary politics would be closely related to a 'total art' of building.

Michael Hamburger, in his book *Reason and Energy*, discusses the implied aesthetic in Expressionist poetry in terms of the programme taken from the English Imagist Manifesto of 1913. It is such a useful document that I have borrowed from it again to relate it this time to the ideas of the architects of the period. Its relevance will, I think, be obvious.

1. To use language of common speech, but to employ always the exact word, not merely a decorative word.
2. To create new rhythms—as an expression of new moods.
3. To allow absolute freedom in the choice of subject.
4. To present an image. We are not a school of painters, but we believe that poets should render particulars exactly and not deal with vague generalities.
5. To produce poetry that is hard and clear, never blurred and indefinite.
6. Finally, most of us believe that concentration is the very essence of poetry.[1]

Looked at objectively this stylistic manifesto sheds a good deal of light upon the German emphasis on the underlying value of the 'idea' or 'image' by which the basic concept in painting, literature and architecture was expressed and freed from inessential details.

After an examination of the architecture and writings of the Expressionists, and with the Imagist Manifesto in mind, the basic principles of the Expressionist architects could be formulated as follows:

The continuation of the *Art Nouveau–Jugendstil* idea of the plasticity and movement of form; but not its curvilinear decorative quality.

Freedom from historical precedent.

Freedom in the experimental use of new materials and constructional techniques.

A belief in the monolithic nature of reinforced concrete as well as its elastic quality. Its usefulness as a sculptural material.

The idea that the internal spaces and external shape of a building had an organic and biological purpose.

The notion that spatial boundaries could be removed by the introduction of large areas of glass—often of varying colours—and that the volume of a building was unlimited and part of the wider cosmic space.

Each building was a total work of art, an artefact complete in itself, a significant object or 'image'. This was related to a belief that architecture was a national phenomenon and each building something of a monument to national taste and pride.

The idea that a building should exhibit a certain clarity of form and emphasis—a marked horizontality, verticality or angularity.

The idea that each part of a building was to be clearly defined architecturally and precisely organized as an integral part of the whole.

Lastly, the embodiment in the concept of a vision of a Utopian society.


*'Die Überwindung des Expressionismus'*

Running parallel to, and in some cases, overlapping Expressionism for some time were the related yet more materialistic ideas of the *Neue Sachlichkeit* (the New Realism, New Objectivity, or New Sobriety as it might be called in English).

This tendency, which was socialistic in origin and aims, developed rapidly under the steadily improving financial and material conditions of the new Germany.[2] It did not have the same concern for the mystical and spiritual aspects of life as Expressionism. It had, Walter Sokel says, in one sense been inherent in Expressionism from its very inception but had by the culmination of the Expressionist phase in fact become powerful enough to supersede it. Sokel goes on to define the term: '*Sachlichkeit* . . . is the attempt to present a "de-emphasised" objective reality, i.e. the dispassionate understanding of the external "world".'[3]

From this objective view of reality a new attitude was to develop in terms of architecture and art. The Expressionist-visionary designs gave way to the functional and the socialistic, the realist-expressionist to the abstract expressionist.

There was soon to be another side to this coin too, a grotesquely shaped idea in the form of

*Idealistische Sachlichkeit* (Idealistic Realism), which, with its revival of Nationalism and traditional modes of life and art, was eventually to destroy both the original revolutionary movements. Its culmination was in the lifeless works of the National Socialist artists and architects, which were as unlike the ideas of the Expressionists—with their basis of a 'perpetual excitement'—as they were contrary to the work of the New Realists.

Germany after 1923–4 was no longer cowering in its own box of frustrations; it had as a nation recovered adequately to apply itself to the social and technical problems at hand. In architecture this meant getting on with the practical job of building, leaving the theoretical notions and paper projects produced during the years immediately after the war behind, or incorporating them as well as possible in the works to be erected in the vast rebuilding programme. The new times demanded that dream architecture should be abandoned for a more technological one.

For a number of reasons the visionary, expressionistic architecture had failed to develop, and the interval of this so-called romantic trend came to an end. For some of course it had been merely an excuse for wild impracticable notions; for others, men like Erich Mendelsohn, Bruno Taut, Hugo Häring and Hans Scharoun, it had certainly served a more serious purpose.[4]

Expressionism had thrived during a period when architecture had been confined to the drawing board; a period when any symbolic effect could be committed to paper but not necessarily built. Quite obviously one of the main reasons for the failure of expressionist architecture was simply that it was too difficult to carry out. I have suggested earlier, in the chapter on Mendelsohn, that even a building as relatively simple as the Einstein Tower was too complex for the builders to construct, and before its completion ship-builders had to be brought in to work out the templates for its curved surfaces. Besides this there was also the realization that the conventional two-dimensional, orthogonal drawing technique was completely inadequate to convey the ideas and construction of such buildings. Most of the Expressionist architects presented their work in the form of sketches, plaster or plasticine models which, although displaying the three-dimensional qualities of the building very well, could not have been a substitute for working drawings.

It was soon found too, that the quality of plasticity implied in the new materials, such as 'ferro-concrete', was not so plastic after all, and glass, which had been advocated by the Berlin 'Glass Chain' group, failed to develop as a constructional material with new architectural possibilities.[5]

Besides all this, and with the basic failure at the level of communication as well as a growing social awareness, the architects of the *avant-garde* in Germany soon turned to the rectangle and to what was termed the new 'rationality'.

168

# Notes on the text

## Chapter 1

1 F. Nietzsche, *Die Geburt der Trageodie aus dem Gieste der Musik*, 1872. English translation in *The authorised English translation of Nietzsche's works* by Oscar Levy (18 vols.), 1909–13. Also in *The birth of tragedy and the genealogy of morals*, New York, 1956.

2 *Encyclopaedia Britannica*, 14th edition, vol. 16; see article on Nietzsche, pp. 432–5. Cf. the views of Wilhelm Michel who defined the idea of 'the new man' as one who 'feels anew the power of fate'.

3 R. Samuel and R. H. Thomas, *Expressionism in German art, life, literature and the theatre: 1910–24*, Cambridge, 1936, p. 71. This English study of the Expressionist phase is invaluable as it presents an objective view of the whole movement.

4 *Ibid.*, p. 71.

5 Quoted in K. Gilbert and H. Kuhn, *A history of esthetics*, London, 1956, p. 520.

6 *Works* (see note 1), vol. 3, p. 68.

7 *Encyclopaedia Britannica*, *loc. cit.*, p. 433.

8 Quoted in Gilbert and Kuhn, *op. cit.*, p. 518. From *Werke*, Grossoktav-Ausgabe, 16 vols., XIV, p. 229f.

9 *Ibid.*, XVI, p. 246.

10 Samuel and Thomas, *op. cit.*, p. 71.

11 *Ecce Homo* is the book in which Nietzsche associates himself directly with Christ, claiming for himself the role of creative redeemer.

12 Quoted by R. J. Hollingdale in his introduction to the Pelican Books translation, *Thus spoke Zarathustra*, Harmondsworth, 1961, p. 20.

13 G. Grosz, *A little yes and a big no*, New York, 1946, p. 82.

14 H. Hoffding, *Sören Kierkegaard als Philosoph*, Stuttgart, 1896.

15 W. Sokel, *The writer in extremis*, Stanford, California, 1959, p. 53.

16 Samuel and Thomas, *op. cit.*, pp. 8–9.

17 O. Benesch, *Edvard Munch*, London, 1960, p. 17.

18 Samuel and Thomas, *op. cit.*, p. 8.

19 Quoted in A. Strindberg, *Eight expressionist plays*, Bantam Books, 1965, in article 'Strindberg the Expressionist' by John Gassner, p. 12.

20 *Ibid.*, the Author's Preface, p. 343.

## Chapter 2

1 Quoted in W. Haftmann, *Painting in the twentieth century*, 2 vols., London, 1960, vol. I, p. 88.

2 R. Samuel and R. H. Thomas, *Expressionism in German art, life, literature and the theatre: 1910–24*, Cambridge, 1936, p. 10. See also Haftmann, *op. cit.*, p. 93. Jethro Bithell in his *Modern German literature: 1880–1950*, London, 1959, points out that the term Expressionism was first used by Otto zur Linde in 1911 with reference to a group of poets associated with the literary review *Charon*.

3 H. Rookmaaker, *Synthetist art theories*, Amsterdam, 1959, p. 95.

4 *Ibid.*, p. 93.

5 Samuel and Thomas, *op. cit.*, p. 10.

6 *The Concise Oxford dictionary*, 3rd revised edition, 1952.

7 Samuel and Thomas, *op. cit.*, p. 11.

8 C. Lake and M. Maillard, *A dictionary of modern painting*, London, 1956 (1958), pp. 95–8.

9 Samuel and Thomas, *op. cit.*, p. 18.

10 A. Soergel, *Dichtung und Dichter der Zeit*, Leipzig, 1927, p. 346. A long extract from Edschmid's *Über den dichterischen Expressionismus* (1917) is given, pp. 346–9. Translation from W. Sokel, *The writer in extremis*, Stanford, 1959, p. 51.

11 The whole question of nihilism in romantic art and architecture is discussed in Hans Sedlmayr's book *Art in crisis*. He refers to a *Verlust der Mitte*—a loss of

the centre—in art. See the author's review for a discussion of this point in *The Christian Graduate*, London, March 1959, pp. 37–8.

12 Samuel and Thomas, *op. cit.*, pp. 17–18.

13 The Futurist Manifesto. See R. Carrieri, *Futurism*, Milan, n.d.; also *Architectural Review*, August–September, 1959, p. 79.

14 Samuel and Thomas, *op. cit.*, p. 16.

15 It is not possible in this study to outline all Gordon Craig's connections with the early Expressionists in Germany. His ideas are put forward in *On the art of theatre*, London, 1911 (1962, p.b.) and in the admirable King Penguin Book, *Edward Gordon Craig*, Harmondsworth, 1948. See Chapter 12 for a discussion on the 'Imagist Manifesto'.

16 *Blast*, no. 2, London, 1915, p. 5.

17 Samuel and Thomas, *op. cit.*, p. 17.

18 *Ibid.*, p. 23.

19 E. Mendelsohn. 'Architecture in a world crisis', in *Three lectures on architecture*, Berkeley and Los Angeles, 1944, p. 8.

20 Introduction by Herbert Read to P. Theone (pseud.) *Modern German art*, Harmondsworth, 1938, pp. 7–8.

21 *Grünewald: the paintings*, London, 1958, p. 120.

22 Ernst Ludwig Kirchner to Curt Valentin, 1937. Quoted in A. H. Barr, *Masters of Modern Art*, New York, 1954, p. 60.

23 P. Selz, *German expressionist painting*, Berkeley and Los Angeles, 1957, p. 67.

24 Lake and Maillard, *op. cit.*, p. 3.

25 Quoted in H. Read, *A History of Modern Painting*, London, 1959, pp. 173–4.

## Chapter 3

1 V. Gregotti, 'Peter Behrens: 1868–1940'. Special issue of *Casabella*, no. 240, p. 5–8, p.vi. (English Digest).

2 From the *Architekturprogramm* issued by the *Arbeitsrat für Kunst* under Taut's signature. Reproduced in U. Conrads, *Programme und Manifeste zur Architektur des 20. Jahrhunderts*, Berlin, 1964, pp. 38–40. Also in U. Conrads and H. G. Sperlich, *Fantastic Architecture*, London, 1963 (original German edition Stuttgart, 1960), pp. 135–6.

3 G. Collins, *Antonio Gaudi*, London, 1960, p. 126, note 55. Collins says further, 'Gaudi's friend Maragell had translated Goethe's works into Catalan and was in great part responsible for his influence in Spain'.

## Chapter 4

1 For a thorough survey of the work of Peter Behrens see *Casabella*, no. 240, 'Numero dedicato a Peter Behrens'.

2 See P. Kremers (ed.) *Peter Behrens*, Essen, 1928, p. 40.

3 Cf. U. Kultermann, *Wassili und Hans Luckhardt: Bauten und Entwürfe*, Tübingen, 1958, pp. 60–1.

## Chapter 5

1 A Dutch translation of this *Werkbund* speech was included in *Wendingen*, no. 11, 1919, pp. 10ff. Almost all translations are from this Dutch version. An extract from this speech is included in the Appendices.

2 See *Das Haus der Freundschaft in Konstantinopel. Ein Wettbewerb deutscher Architekten*. Introduction by Theodor Heuss, Munich 1918. The competition was won by German Bestelmeyer. Other entries included those from Peter Behrens, Paul Bonatz, August Endell and Bruno Taut.

3 H. F. Garten, *Modern German drama*, London, 1959, p. 85.

4 H. G. Scheffauer, 'Hans Poelzig', *Architectural Review*, October 1923, pp. 122–7. See also T. Heuss, *Hans Poelzig: Lebensbild eines Baumeisters*, Tübingen, 1939 (1955), section entitled 'Theater der Fünftausend', pp. 68–75; and T. Heuss, *Hans Poelzig: Bauten und Entwürfe*, Berlin, 1939.

5 Quoted in F. Stahl, 'Hans Poelzig' in *Wasmuth's Monatshefte für Baukunst*, no. 4, 1919–20, p. 4.

6 *Wendingen*, *op. cit.*, p. 7.

7 *Ibid.*, p. 11.

8 See Heuss, *op. cit.*, pp. 90–6.

9 *Architectural Review*, July 1939, p. 39.

## Chapter 6

1 V. Gregotti, 'Peter Behrens, 1868–1940', in *Casabella*, no. 240, p.v. (English Digest).

2 B. Taut, *Modern Architecture*, London, 1929, p. 92. In this book Taut writes about the postwar situation in Germany and of the 'havoc in the mental attitude of the public'. He goes on, 'small wonder that in these circumstances, the architects desirous of paving the way for a new architecture, could at first find no other basis but in themselves. Small wonder that they felt forced to give the uttermost and noisiest vent to their own feelings, if only to be

heard at all, preaching and rhapsodising about unity which neither existed nor could be evolved. That this state of mind, known as "Expressionism" was abandoned by the best of them as far back as 1923 (the time of the inflation) can only be valued at its true worth by those familiar with the conditions in Germany which then prevailed.' (p. 93).

3 For a discussion of the *Arbeitsrat für Kunst*, see the following publications. N. Pevsner, 'Finsterlin and some others', *Architectural Review*, November 1962, pp. 353–7; G. Lindahl, 'Von der Zukunftskathedrale bis zur Wohnmaschine' in *Idea and Form*, Stockholm, 1959, pp. 226–82; U. Conrads and H. G. Sperlich, *Fantastic architecture*, London, 1963.

4 B. Taut, 'Ein Architektur-Programm', reproduced in U. Conrads, *Programme und Manifeste zur Architektur des 20. Jahrhunderts*, Berlin, 1964, pp. 38–40.

5 Quote from Conrads and Sperlich, *op. cit.*, p. 138.

6 Quoted in Pevsner, *op. cit.*, p. 356.

7 Translation used in Conrads and Sperlich, *op. cit.*, p. 139.

8 See U. Kultermann, *Wassili und Hans Luckhardt: Bauten und Entwürfe*, Tübingen, 1958.

9 See G. Platz, *Die Baukunst der Neuesten Zeit*, Berlin, 1927, pp. 382 and 532.

10 J. Joedicke, 'Haering at Garkau', *Architectural Review*, May 1960, pp. 313–18: p. 317.

11 *Ibid.*, p. 318.

12 Quoted in P. Johnson, *Mies van der Rohe*, New York, 1947 (revised 1953), p. 187.

13 *Ibid.*, p. 187.

14 *Ibid.*, p. 187.

15 *Ibid.*, p. 188.

16 *Idem.*, p. 313.

17 W. Müller-Wulckow, *Bauten der Arbeit, Wohnbauten und Siedlungen* and *Bauten der Gemeinschaft*, Königstein im Taunus, and Leipzig, 1925–9. These books and the magazines of the time indicate the variety of prewar and postwar German architecture and clearly show the development of the 'functionalist' stream side-by-side with what might be termed the conservative expressionist architecture. Platz's book, *op. cit.*, indicates the variety of work produced in Germany since 1895 and includes photographs of engineering structures. This book, together with Behne's *Moderne Zweckbau* (published 1926) recently reissued (Berlin, 1964), give a valuable commentary on the state of architecture in the early part of the twentieth century in Germany.

## Chapter 7

1 See *Frühlicht* article 'Glashausbriefe' in B. Taut, *Frühlicht 1920–22: Eine Folge für die Verwirklichung des neuen Baugedankens*, Berlin, 1963, pp. 18–19.

2 P. Scheerbart, *Glasarchitektur*, Berlin, 1914, p. 11.

3 It is interesting to compare the design submitted by Taut in collaboration with Walter Gunther and K. Schutz, for the *Chicago Tribune* Tower competition. Illustrated in *The International Competition for a New Administrative Building for the Chicago Tribune: 1922*, Chicago, 1923. See illustration on page 93.

4 B. Taut, *Modern architecture*, London, 1929, p. 9.

5 *Ibid.*, p. 9.

## Chapter 8

1 Quoted from Jacques Couëlle, 'L'architecture naturelle', in *Art* (Numero hors-série de l'Architecture d'Aujourd'hui), Boulogne-sur-Seine, 1946, pp. 33–6. See also the article on visionary architecture 'l'architecture allégorique' by Marcel Jean in the same volume. Cf. Th. Wijdeveld, 'Architectonische Phantasien in de Wereld der Kristallen', in the Dutch magazine *Wendingen*, No. 12, 1924.

2 H. Finsterlin, 'Innenarchitektur', *Frühlicht*, Magdeburg, no. 2, 1921–2 (reproduced in B. Taut, *Frühlicht 1920–22*, Berlin, 1963, pp. 105–9: p. 107). The German is difficult to translate into English: *'Im Innenraum des neuen Hauses wird man sich nicht nur als Insasse einer märchenhaften Kristalldruse fühlen, sondern als interner Bewohner eines Organismus, wandernd von Organ zu Organ, ein gebender und empfangender Symbiote eines "fossilen Riesenmutterleibes".'*

3 In a letter to the writer.

4 Otto Conzelmann, 1949, reproduced in the catalogue for the exhibition *60 Jahre Finsterlin: Querschnitt durch sein Schaffen*, Stuttgart, 1964.

5 H. Finsterlin. 'Der achte Tag', in *Frühlicht*, Berlin, no. 11, 1920; *op. cit.*, pp. 52–9: p. 52. See Appendix 3 for a partial translation.

6 C. J. Blaauw, 'Architectonisch Droomspiel', in *Wendingen*, no. 3, 1924, p. 3.

7 A note in *Architectural Review*, January 1963, p. 5. See also N. Pevsner, 'Finsterlin and some others', *Architectural Review*, November, 1962, pp. 353–7.

## Chapter 9

1 From 'Reflections on new architecture', in *Erich Mendelsohn: structures and sketches*, London, 1924, p. 3. See Appendix 2 for full text.

2 R. Banham, 'Mendelsohn', *Architectural Review*, August, 1954, pp. 85–93: p. 85.

3 E. Mendelsohn. 'Background to Design', *Architectural Forum*, April 1953, p. 106.

4 In a letter to the writer, December 1961.

5 This pertinent remark comes from Mendelsohn's article 'Background to Design', *op. cit.*, p. 106.

6 N. Pevsner, 'Mendelsohn by Himself', *Architectural Review*, March 1962, pp. 161–3. This is a review article of the book compiled by Mendelsohn's widow, consisting of personal letters to her from her husband: *Briefe eines Architekten*, Munich, 1961.

7 Mendelsohn, 'Background to Design', *op. cit.*, p. 106.

8 *Ibid.*, p. 106.

9 *Ibid.*, p. 106.

10 *Ibid.*, p. 107.

11 See for example M. Robertson, *Laymen and the new architecture*, London, 1925, p. 75.

12 A. Whittick, *Eric Mendelsohn*, 2nd edn., London, 1956, p. 57.

13 E. Mendelsohn, 'Architecture of our own times', reproduced in the *Architectural Association Journal*, June 1930, pp. 5–16: p. 7. The lecture was given 19 May 1930.

14 'Reflections on new architecture', *op. cit.*, p. 3.

15 All quotations from Le Corbusier's *Towards a new architecture*, London, 1927 (1946 edn.).

16 'Reflections on New Architecture', *op. cit.*, p. 3.

17 E. Mendelsohn, 'Architecture in a World Crisis' in *Three lectures on architecture*, Berkeley and Los Angeles, 1944, p. 13.

18 A. Behne, *Der Moderne Zweckbau*, Munich, 1923, p. 39. Recently republished in paperback form by Ullstein, Berlin, 1964.

19 *Ibid.*, p. 38.

20 A. A. Lecture, *op. cit.*, p. 12.

21 *Briefe eines Architekten*, *op. cit.*, p. 57.

22 A. Huxley, 'Puritanism in art', *The Studio*, March 1930, pp. 200–2: p. 201.

23 *Ibid.*, p. 201.

24 From *Bauwelt*, 1961, no. 41–2, p. 1184. See Appendix 2 for original German version.

25 A. A. Lecture, *op. cit.*, p. 16.

26 *Ibid.*, p. 5.

27 *Ibid.*, p. 5.

28 *Ibid.*, p. 6.

29 E. Mendelsohn, 'The Three Dimensions of Architecture—their symbolic significance', in *Symbols and values* (13th Symposium on Science, Philosophy and Religion), New York, 1954, Chapter XVII, pp. 235–54: p. 252.

30 *Ibid.*, p. 253.

31 C. H. Reilly, *Scaffolding in the sky*, London, 1938, p. 292.

## Chapter 10

1 J. P. Mieras and F. R. Yerbury, *Dutch architecture of the XXth century*, London, 1926, p. xi.

2 Quoted from a review by R. Newbolt of Wattjes books *Nieuw-Nederlandsche Bouwkunst* (Amsterdam, 1923 and 1929) in the *Architectural Review*, October 1931, p. 109.

3 J. Blijstra, *Netherlands architecture since 1900*. Amsterdam 1960.

4 *Wendingen* was first issued in January 1918. The editor was H. Th. Wijdeveld, and the editorial board consisted of Blaauw, Endt, van den Eynde, Kramer, Lauwericks, van Loghem, Holst and Granpré Molière. It was published for *Het genootschap Architectura et Amicitia*.

5 A special number of *Wendingen* on Frank Lloyd Wright appeared in 1921 and a special seven-part volume, in three languages, in 1925.

6 Quoted in N. Pevsner, 'Frank Lloyd Wright's Peaceful Penetration of Europe', *Architects' Journal*, vol. 89, 1939, pp. 731–4: p. 732.

7 See an expanded discussion of the work of van't Hoff and Wils in R. Banham, *Theory and design in the first machine age*, London, 1960, pp. 54ff.

8 H. Poelzig, 'Rede Gehouden ter Gelegenheid van de Harleving van den Werkbund' ('Lecture held on the occasion of the revival of the Werkbund'), in *Wendingen*, no. 11, 1919. See Appendix 1 for partial translation.
   Articles: on Finsterlin in *Wendingen*, no. 3, 1924. Mendelsohn, *Wendingen*, no. 10, 1920; Hoffmann, *Wendingen*, nos. 8–9, 1920; and Klimt, no. 2, 1920.

9 The most comprehensive guide to de Klerk's work is given in *Wendingen*. The more important articles being, P. H. Endt, 'Amsterdamse School', no. 7, 1918; de Bazel, 'Onze tijd en het werk van M. de Klerk', no. 2, 1919; 'In uitbreiding "Zuid" te Amsterdam', no. 4, 1923; 'En geheel gewijd aan de onuitgevoerde architectonische projecten van

architect M. de Klerk . . .', nos. 4 and 5, 1924;
P. Kramer, 'De Bouwwerken van M. de Klerk', nos.
9 and 10, 1924; an article on interiors and furniture
by de Klerk, no. 10, 1925.

10 These portraits are reproduced in *Wendingen*, no 7, 1924.

11 *Wendingen*, nos. 4 and 5, 1924, p. 3.

12 J. Ruskin, *Lectures on architecture and painting*, London, 1905, p. 105.

13 *Ibid.*, p. 36.

14 The whole of *Wendingen*, no. 8, 1918, is devoted to the work in the Park Meerwijk, Bergen. See article, H. Th. Wijdeveld, 'Het Park Meerwijk te Bergen'.

15 Wijdeveld article, *ibid.*, p. 8.

16 *Ibid.*, p. 8.

## Chapter 11

1 Quoted in 'Rudolf Steiner and anthroposophy', a pamphlet issued by the Anthroposophical Society of Great Britain, p. 4. See R. Steiner, *The story of my life*, London, 1928, p. 11.

2 R. Steiner, *The story of my life*, p. 252.

3 Pamphlet, p. 1.

4 In K. Bayes, 'The search for new forms in architecture', a lecture given to commemorate the Rudolf Steiner Centenary on 8 March 1961. (unpublished typewritten copy, kindly lent to the writer).

5 H. L. C. Jaffé, *de Stijl*, Amsterdam, 1956.

6 Alma Mahler Werfel, *The bridge is love*, London, 1959.

7 R. Steiner, *Ways to a new style in architecture*, London, 1927, p. 42–3.

8 See chapter entitled, 'Architecture in Accord with Man' in *The faithful thinker: centenary essays on the work and thought of Rudolf Steiner* (ed. A. C. Harwood), London, 1961, pp. 163–78, etc. Also an article was published in *L'Architettura*, no. 81, 1962, showing two buildings designed in the 'Steiner style' by Bayes—a school at East Grinstead and a house at Camphill, Yorks.

9 Bayes, lecture, p. 8; see note 4.

10 H. van de Velde. *Les formules de la beauté architectonique moderne*, Brussels, 1923, p. 64.

11 Bayes, lecture, p. 8; see note 4.

12 Steiner, *Ways to a new style in architecture*, p. 21.

13 *Ibid.*, p. 21.

14 Quoted in *The Goetheanum*, Dornach, 1961, p. 7, (pamphlet).

15 Steiner, *Ways to a new style in architecture*, p. 11.

16 *Ibid.*, p. 10.

17 Steiner, *Ways to a new style in architecture*, p. 54.

18 M. Wilson, 'Colour, science and thinking', in *Rudolf Steiner*, pp. 141–52, p. 147.

19 For a further discussion see H. Read, *A concise history of modern painting*, London, 1959, pp. 48, 94, 95, etc.
Also see for a more detailed discussion of colour symbolism and modern painting, particularly in relation to French painting of the turn of the century, H. R. Rookmaaker, *Synthetist art theories*, Amsterdam, 1959.

20 H. Read, *A concise history of modern painting*, London, 1959, p. 48.

21 Steiner, *Ways to a new style in architecture*, pp. 54–5.

22 *Ibid.*, p. 55.

## Chapter 12

1 M. Hamburger, *Reason and energy: studies in German literature*, London, 1957, p. 214.

2 The German *Deutsche-Mark* for example was stabilized in 1924 after having been reduced in 1923 to the absurd value of 100,000,000 DM's for five shillings (i.e., one dollar).

3 W. H. Sokel, *The writer in extremis*, Stanford, California, 1959, p. 161.

4 Hans Scharoun has since the 'golden twenties' always stood by his idea of 'organic building'. Since then he has produced schemes—many for competitions—that might still be termed Expressionist. Since the end of the Second World War his work has become increasingly acceptable to his fellow architects both inside Germany and abroad and he has now won a number of important competitions instead of being placed second. Examples of his work can be seen at Lünen—school; at Stuttgart—blocks of apartments known as 'Romeo and Juliet'; Berlin—the new Philharmonic Hall, etc.

5 That is, except for the introduction and rather limited use of glass blocks and glass-concrete construction.

# Appendices

# Appendix 1

## Hans Poelzig

### Lecture held on the occasion of the revival of the *Werkbund* 1919

It must be stressed that the *Werkbund* originated from a spiritual, not from an economic movement. Its character has faded under the influence of all sorts of political and economic enterprises, and it is about time that its essence should be exposed again in all its clarity.

Art and handicraft are the two foundations on which the work of the *Werkbund* has to be based. They are meant to be one and the same thing; but a good handicraft and a great art can only exist when they originate from a pure intention; human failures are the causes of imperfections in art and handicraft.

I want to define handicraft here as something purely spiritual, a spiritual inclination or mood, and not the perfect skill in a certain trade. What we mean by handicraft—and essentially the same refers to art —is the urge to create forms with great absorption and love, and in the meantime no attention will be paid to economic exploitation of the work. This is the principal difference between this work and all purely industrial enterprises.

Industry, in a wider meaning, has to do with technical things only, and is guided by economic principles in the first place. Art and handicraft, however, can only thrive when the urge to create forms is definite, while economic considerations during these creations set the bounds.

Art and handicraft create things which, once finished, have eternal value, and which cannot be destroyed without serious damage. The artist or the artisan who does not want to make things with eternal value does not deserve his name. Their field approaches that of industry, where taste plays a major part. Taste, however, is subject to laws, which have been set beforehand by achievements of higher standard. It works according to formulas which are known to be pleasantly and easily applied. However, an artistic product of strong character resists rightly to be called tasteful. So, if the *Werkbund* does not want to be merely a mediator or instigator of industrial art, which is subject to fashion and change, it will have to turn to the primitive and start building from that stage, i.e. it has to occupy itself with true art and true handicraft. I have the impression that people always make the same mistake. They equalize products of technique on a purely industrial basis, with handicraft products. The technical product requires practical technical considerations and it will lose its value immediately after the production of a technically more perfect, practical and cheaper product. The old product will be cleared and rightly deprecated, because its value is merely technical–commercial. Handicraft and art products have eternal value. A wonderfully shaped baroque chest of drawers does not in the least lose its value, because a more modern chest is more practical, light and cheaper. Those pieces of furniture, however, which owe their existence to technical and economic considerations, e.g. American office furniture, lose their value when one tries to embellish them by means of an artistic shape. From all these mistakes originated the fatal conception of industrial art. I still cannot see any difference between most of the products of the last twenty years and those of the past. They are still trying to achieve something in a formalistic way by means of an approach from the outside.

Industry has to limit itself to those things which are nothing else but practical. They create their own forms by slowly divesting themselves of all the superfluous and unpractical, and they will soon get a current form, which, however, originated in a different way to that of the artistic handicraft, and which can be fixed apart from economical considerations, at its best by means of prudence and taste.

It is self-evident that I would be wrong in deprecating the achievements in our technical industries. As a matter of fact, work there is for the greater part more unselfish and more businesslike, without a tendency to satisfy personal vanities, than in the field of art and even of half-art.

The cheap fame by sensation, which comes over and harms so many of our young artists, does not exist there. My only intention is to denote, as far as possible, some boundaries, in order to clarify my point. The wide field of architecture touches on the borderlines of pure technique and adopts its technical results, which originated in a technical–scientific way, observing its commercial practicability. Although the attempted interference of architecture in the purely technical field, in the construction of motor-cars etc., and all sorts of machines, is often vain and wrong—although even in building steel bridges, the most perfect construction only comes from technical and economic principles—yet the construction itself, originating solely from scientific and technical considerations in the first place, is not free from aridity.

In this respect most of the water-towers, silos and sky-scrapers are not buildings which can be compared with the aqueducts, fortifications and granaries of the past. It is necessary that the artistic element is present which makes use of the technical possibilities, but which is in itself able to shape the form of the building.

The average engineer will build a bad water-tower, a bad factory, as far as the form is concerned; the average architect, who thinks to do his duty by only working with the outside in mind, often an even worse water-tower or factory.

All relatively perishable things which have to be superseded immediately by better technical achievements when the time comes, can and may only be designed by the engineer, but all those buildings which are to remain for even 30–50 years as buildings, must get a form which originates from the architectonic urge for creation of the artist, with strict observance of the technical principles. Our 'building-skill' has, where technique is concerned, better and richer possibilities than in the

Middle Ages; it is, however, just as possible as in the Middle Ages to give the concrete or steel construction of a wood warehouse a form which is in agreement with the essence of its construction. That compromises only deteriorate and lead to impurity of style is evident in the technical buildings in which one tried to follow the old accepted rhythmical laws, as for example of the Antique, or in those which try to hide themselves behind an architectonic, rhythmic mask, which is, however, in contradiction to the logical coherence of the applied construction.

Also the construction of our houses cannot be developed from technical-hygienic principles or often intellectual or scientific considerations only, as is the case with mechanically made objects of practical use, which, after having done their duty, are thrown away. The houses of people require that observance must be paid for senses of value, which cannot be given by mere constructions however practicable they may be. We can better be impracticable as long as we can achieve that by our creation a beam of light will fall into the human soul.

It will be clear to everyone with common sense that the character of our modern constructing methods is in contradiction to the forms of Antiquity in its flourishing period. Our methods aim towards an analysis of forces, to the solution and arrangement of them, and they are therefore closer to the medieval conception than the Antique. I say the medieval, not the Gothic, because a comparison with the complicated terminology of form of the Gothic in its flourishing period will only lead to confusion. The approaching time of poverty seems to me an opportunity to divest architecture of impurities in style. The means are few and compel us to limitations. Don't let us follow Schinkel who stressed the adoption of perfect Antique forms, but who could not on commercial grounds give an equal appreciation of antique and modern materials.

A pure architecture needs strict forms and discipline, but not a mixture of different rhythmical principles, which is meant to be considered as richness of imagination, but which is nothing but cheap fancy. Architecture is the product of a national state of mind, and the average deplorable architecture of the German towns during the last few years was a result of the psychic corruption of a nation, which desired only material gains, a nation which had lost the psychic connection with its native soil, and for that reason did not have a native soil any more. Our aim is to reconnect them again. We can only reach that by means of a change of attitude, by the resuscitation of satisfaction from labour.

All palliatives, which only pertained to form, failed and had to fail. They were limited to the outside, the decorative, and, moreover, where commercial considerations and the spirit of trade prevails, there every artistic initiative, based on inner inspiration, will die.

But we can only achieve an architecture as an *ars magna* where the same total change of mind has taken place, where the conviction has been established that we have to create for eternity.

However, we have to understand that a great art, lest it deteriorate, must have inspiring content, and must have a tight connection with the soul of the people. We must be indifferent to the commercial value which has been imposed on works of art.

We can only achieve a fundamental improvement when architects get an education in building works of art, and when every tie, unbearable for the artist who is ahead of his time, can be broken. It is a difficult problem and cannot be solved by theories that are usually protective and so retrospective. To the contrary, we have to prefer every promising creative conception, which is justified by the architectonic-musical character of its surroundings only, to a sentimental, retrospective one. . . .

*Translated from the Dutch by Hugo van der Wolf.*

# Appendix 2

## Erich Mendelsohn

### From *Reflections on New Architecture* (written at the Front 1914-17)

*In general*

Architecture is the only tangible expression of space of which the human spirit is capable. Architecture seizes upon space, encompasses space and is space itself. Out of the three-dimensional infinitude of universal space—which is beyond human conception—Architecture brings us, by means of its spatial delimitation, the concept of room and bulk.

Its values are those of space and surface and it is founded wholly upon mathematical actuality. The geometry of space, the law of the seizure and the penetration of space, of corporeal determination and of constructed bulk, embrace all fabrics: the simplest equation from the cube to the sphere, and the highest, arising from some cosmic blossoming-forth.

The living quality of architecture depends upon sensuous seizure by means of touch and sight: upon the terrestrial cohesion of mass, upon the superterrestrial liberty of light.

It is light that first gives movement to mass and sublimates it to a supersensuous expression of dynamic and rhythmic agitation.

It is light that first rounds out mathematical precision and space consciousness to the freedom, independence and law of architectonic creation.

Out of its own laws architecture lays down the conditions that govern its active masses:

The *dynamic* condition—the movement of space—to visualize its linear elements by means of its contours; the *rhythmic* condition—to visualize the relation of the masses—by means of the projection of surfaces; and the *static* condition—the equalization of movement to visualize this as elements of construction by means of ground plan and section.

Architecture determines its own standard from time to time, a standard that instinctively apperceives, compares and coordinates, a standard that scientifically tests, measures, divides and proves.

This standard, by virtue of the objectivity inherent in its corporeal detachment, and its absolute attitude, serves to resolve mysterious secrets into predestined law and order.

Closely related to this law and order we find the extra-human and inconceivable, things that bow and erect themselves, that burrow beneath and overtop one another, in grotesque accentuation, from the building blocks of the child to the tower spawned by chaos.

Miracles of measurement, of consummated coincidences and harmonies as well as layers and series of inspired proportions are discovered; mutual corrections and equalities of will, sacred things that the law of creation bestows upon its creature, and the artist upon his creation. Profound necessity decrees that all artistic creation should be subject to the same stern law of life.

*The inner and outer wall*

The outer wall acts upon the visible universe: its physical compactness operates upon the illimitableness of space. It is part of the builded law, the united voice of spatial and constructive demands, a section in space towards a certain direction. Its law of limitations is imposed by the building as a whole.

Its decomposition is subject to the law of superficies in space. The outer wall collects light, in order to let it penetrate fully through its openings.

The inner wall determines the centre of gravity of the room by means of its limitations. This wall is an independent surface, and is related only to its companion walls, with the floor and with the ceiling.

Its decomposition brings about the sliding of surface into surface. When this wall happens to be a functional part of the construction, of a framework, of a vault or a span—a burden-bearer or a burden-conductor—then it becomes subject to a structural inhibition.

The unique nature of architectonic space conditions the unique quality of its effects. Its final, consummate expression is independent of decoration and dress.

Its being fettered to material media implies no lessening of its innate worth; architecture demands freedom of space in order to stretch its limbs, it demands the freedom of the Will-to-build in order to assert itself.

It portends a transformation into the future, it becomes a great event governed by new laws.

Architecture is the expression of the will of an epoch and of the spirit of that epoch. It binds its single law to the fate of a nation.

It bears witness to this nation's needs and hopes, its achievements, longings and its God. It bears witness to origin, to growth and decay. Architecture is proof of its inherited, its nourished and its spontaneous, self-engendered will. It is a document of its political history, its spiritual mission, its intrinsic culture.

The singleness of its general operation corresponds to the responsibility of all architectonic work; the reshaping of vision into actuality, the uniting of free creation with expedient objectivity. Only the well-rounded, self-contained personality will be able alike to dominate intuition and calculation.


## From 'The Problem of a New Architecture' (Lecture, 1919)

All that has been achieved in the creation of new architectural form, since the great autonomous efflorescence of medieval architecture, and even during the most fruitful period of the baroque, down to

182

the days of our own artistic exhaustion, is based in principle upon the inherited forms and traditions of antique building art.

Precisely as there is no longer any connection between the principle of the antique world with its simple load and support, and the Gothic principle with column and vault—both in the manner of construction and of ornamental architectonic expression—so must we clearly recognize the fact that the first iron girder inspired and exalted a feeling of liberation akin to that which the medieval masters felt when they had conquered the antique principle of construction by means of the vault.

It is only from this point of departure that one is able to realize that the decisive features of the new constructive principle must be discovered again and again.

The regulation of our static sensation in accordance with the tensile power of reinforced concrete, instead of, as hitherto, with the principle of direct load and support, necessitates a long and gradual approach and evolution. It is therefore particularly urgent to discover and emphasize this antithesis in order to be able to visualize the breadth and extent of this great change.

Out of the columns and marble beams of the Greek temple,

Out of the pillars and stone vaults of the Gothic cathedral,

Evolves the girder rhythm of iron halls.

The balancing of the load practised by the ancients, the elevation of the load practised by the medievals, are succeeded by the dynamic tension of construction in steel and concrete.

It was in accordance with modern commercial exploitation that industry and manufacture should first seize upon all possibilities of profit afforded by the new material, and utilizing it for technical and economic purposes and for tools and machines, unconsciously create centres of energy for the new and coming form, and by virtue of the technical auxiliaries of transportation, produce the first fabric constructed in the new spirit. It is here that material speaks and enforces its own verdict.

But one more step and the connection with architectonic form is established. It is unthinkable, or would so appear, that the compact energies of iron as employed in the machine and in engines of transportation, should remain without any influence upon the same material which has already been fettered to use in a tectonic or structural sense.

It is therefore small wonder that the decisive problems of modern building should proceed from the industrial world. This paramountcy of industrial ends in architecture is based upon the unequivocal nature of the purpose in view and upon actual paternity.

This purpose and paternity can serve architecture only as a portal, not as a goal of its own development.


## From 'Dynamics and Function' (Lecture 1923)

In speaking of 'dynamics' we must never interpret this term in the sense of a mechanical operation or movement, for this is wholly and solely the province of the machine.

To translate 'dynamics' into such terms as 'vital force', 'vitality' or 'emotion' is at best ambiguous. Such indefinable values, deeply rooted in the blood of the race, are really no special perquisite of our times. A feeling of vital force is the inspiration and the urge behind every productive act. In principle it signifies nothing more than the twin concepts: gifts and personality, or genius and will. It is in direct proportion to the productive force as well as to the aesthetic achievement. It is independent of time and place—one need think only of a few great examples such as that of ancient Egypt, the temple at Karnak, or one in the Gothic North, the Marienkirche at Danzig.

But if we wish to confine ourselves to dynamics as the logical expression for the movement of the forces indwelling in the materials of building, that is, if we regard the building itself as the expression of actual needs and of these forces, then, in contrast to the machine, we obtain for 'movement' a clear vision, extended into the Absolute. And this vision or picture is the same for all building periods in which originality held sway.

Seen in this light, the construction principle of the Greek temple with its load and support, and the Gothic principle with pillar and vault, are nothing more than the movement and counter-movement of these immanent forces.

The individual force is always static, but the play and interplay of forces is always dynamic.

The building material of our day, that is to say, steel, is constantly, through the revolutionary play of the forces of tension and pressure, revealing the most astonishing movement to the initiated, movements absolutely incomprehensible to the layman.

It is our task to find an architectonic expression for these forces of mobility, and by means of architectonic form to establish an equipoise for these tensions, as well as to master the inner forces which are bent upon expressing themselves in outer forms.

Precisely as in the case of dynamics, we are confronted here by several points of departure when considering the concept of 'open function'. The tracing-back of all forms of phenomena to the rudimentary geometrical basis, is the first essential of all original beginnings. Knowledge of the elements has always been the first condition of creation.

When, however, this two-dimensional knowledge is transferred to or translated into space without a living relation to the third dimension of depth—depth which first creates a spatial organism out of the elementary spatial concepts of cube, sphere and cylinder—then we are in peril of succumbing to purely intellectual construction.

The danger of an unbridled temperament in the matter of dynamics corresponds here to the equally great danger of an all-too-conscious abstraction. Plethora as well as anaemia are both danger zones for vital creation.

When principle becomes an end in itself, then 'form *per se*' no longer signifies architecture. This is a law that applies to all time, not only to Expressionism and Constructivism.

In contradistinction to theoretical form, a claw or forceps type of crane is, for example, an unmistakable prehensile organ—a typical instance of pure mechanical function.

This regular concept of functioning is translated in building construction to function in the mathematical sense of sequential dependence. Thus, whilst the activity of the machine—its seizing, pulling, tearing movements—represents a pure utilitarian function, and function in building represents nearly mathematical sequence and effect, function in architecture can signify only the spatial and formal dependence from postulates of use, of the material and the construction.

For these reasons it seems impossible to transfer the utilitarian or 'purpose-function' of the machine in any form or manner to space as embodied in architecture, or to plant its organization upon the organism of architecture.

We architects must from the very beginning subject our plans to the demands and limits imposed upon them by material and constructional considerations. We must regard them as the preliminary conditions upon which the organization of an entire building depends. But we must know that they are only one component of the productive process. The other component lies in the capacity to create the architectonic expression for these elementary conditions, that is to say, to translate the technical conditions into spatial concretions, and to bring them in mutual dependence upon one another unto the last detail. That is to say, we must bring about that harmony which has produced such marvels of proportion in the best buildings of all ages—that wonderful re-transference of emotional phenomena or processes to mathematic quantities and geometrical relationships.

Thus, two components are necessary for architectural creation. The first is that of the intellect, of the brain, of the organizing machine, which, however, is often subconsciously illumined by lightning-like, visionary glimpses of the possibilities of spatial expression. The second is that which has to do with the creative impulse, proceeding upon the basis of the antecedent organization, of blood, temperament, the sensuous nature and of organic feeling.

It is only the union of both components which leads to mastery over the elements of space or room; the elements resident in the mass tangible to the senses and the supersensual element of light. It is only their union that leads to the accentuation or intensification of mass or to its balance.

It does not matter whether this end be striven for in a harmonic order, that is to say, side by side, or whether in sequence or succession of the separate masses, or whether they be sought for in counter-point order, that is to say, in the augmentation or countermovement of the parts of the mass.

But the living joy of creation, the 'spatial-joy' (Raumlust) of the architect, is something which will spring into life only from the mutual, alternating relations between function and dynamics, between reality and unreality, consciousness and unconsciousness, between reason and emotion, between limitation and infinity. It is alone the union of these things which brings us mastery over the elements of room and bulk, and leads us to the clarified architectonic organism.

*Translated by H. G. Scheffauer.*

## 'Zur Eröffnung des Kino "Universum", 1931'

Kino?

Filmspiel, Theater der Bewegung!

Bewegung ist Leben.

Wirkliches Leben ist echt, einfach und wahr, deshalb keine Pose, keine Rührmätzchen.

Im Film nicht, nicht auf der Leinwand, nicht im Bau.

Zeigt, was drinsteht, was dran ist, was draufgeht. — Bühnenhaus? — Keine Spur!

Elevator für die Bildleinwand, wenn der Sketch den Film ablöst. — Reklameturm, Scheinarchitektur? —

Im Gegenteil! Entlüftungsschlot (Luftwechsel dreimal in der Stunde), herausgerückt in Richtung Kurfürstendamm:

Den haltgemacht: Universum — die ganze Welt! — Palastfassaden? — Und die Rentabilität: Läden machen Geld, Büros beleben und schaffen Publikum.

Säuleneingang für Mondäne?

Maul, gross aufgesperrt mit Lichtflut und Schaugepränge.

Denn — Du sollst hinein, Ihr alle — ins Leben, zum Film, an die Kasse!

Dommkuppeln? Wozu! Schildkrötendach, Schutzwölbung der schrägen Decke, schrägzu auf die Bildwand — Aha! Kamera!

Richtig!

Bildleinwand — die Aussenwelt.

Filmbild — das bunte Leben, Tränen, Zirkus und Meermondschein.

Wir Zuschauer — tausend, zweitausend Objektive, die aufsaugen und reflektieren, vergnügt sind oder erleben.

Also kein Rokokoschloss für Buster Keaton keine Stucktorten für Potemkin und Scapa Flow.

Aber keine Angst auch!

Keine trockene Sachlichkeit, keine Raumangst lebensmüder Gehirnakrobaten — Phantasie!

Phantasie — aber kein Tollhaus — beherrscht durch Raum, Farbe und Licht.

Unter dem schwebenden Ring des Foyers verschwindet Dir die Strasse, unter dem Scheinwerferkegel seiner Decke das Dunstlicht des Abends.

Dann — links oder rechts vorbei am Leuchtturm der Kasse in das Helldunkel des Umgangs — Hier triffst Du 'sie' sicher.

Duck, Dich in Spannung!

Kompressor!

Aber dann volle Tour.

Alle Flächen, Kurven, Orgelbänder und Lichtrollen der Decke sausen zur Leinwand über das Medium der Musik ins flimmernde Bild — ins Universum.

# Appendix 3

## Hermann Finsterlin

### An extract from *The Eighth Day* 1920

A spiral bourgeoning a thousandfold
Ploughs out its path into unmeasured Alls.
And Caryatids find in hope a hold,
Whilst clouds catch up their burden as it falls.

At the wayside cross of blessed radiance,
Nestled within the eternal decree
Of omnipresent audience,
The mandate of selfhood circles free.

Tell me what love is, what faith, and the iron will of hope—and I will tell you what it means to build: to bring the seventh day of creation one wave further in the tidal chain that lovingly toys with eternity. There is no greater Affirmer than the true builder. Everything about him is expansion, pressing outwards,—the more rhythmical, harmonious and healthy the pulse of his soul, the more perfect and inimitable will be the superstructure [*Überleib*] he sets upon the world's countenance, like a victorious seal upon his existence. Manifold flows the creature out of the cornucopia of the universal spirit: soul-twins, who despite perfect concordance of sensibility, utterly diverge in their power of expression; soul-constitutions, that on the plane of incarnation split into iridescent fragments.—These partial smeltings are the cause that not every creature can and must be a creator; that that giving, fashioning for each other was born, which remodelled the adrogyne spirit in two sexes, high above the physical sexus. There is much that but slumbers: let us be Awakeners, Brothers, gentle but strong awakeners, that the little we have be not reduced even more, under the curse of a jealous god.—Building is everything—love, generation, struggle, movement, suffering, parents and child, and the most sacred symbol of everything that is holy. I tell you, such a shape must sound out like the granite body of Memnon, when the sun's waking gaze caresses it; like the Pied Piper's blossoming prayer,—such a vessel must have its perfumes, which inscribe it into the organ of the godhead out of myriad similes,—and the echo of the world's song must cling to the gracious modelling of the joy-breathing new bodies, that bourgeon forth like tardy offspring of the hoary earth. Generations have their see-sawing periods,—the race of the tectons had grown listless and hang-dog,—the grandchildren of the kings, so it seems to me, should rise again,—the prototypes stand charged with energy in the glassy atmosphere of the world of today, they yearn for their redeemers, in whose veins the primal enthusiasm flows like the hybrid of approaching death.—Do you profess, Friends?

Somewhere in the All the god forgot to blink, and the tear-spring of his joys dissolves like the voice of his pulse, building stalagmitic wonders on the mosaic of the sacred earth.—In the maternal body of our world a seismotic foetus is active and decks her skin with his multilimbed filigree, a relief for enraptured perspects, a toothed plate in whose clearings the breath of the leaping earth starts up an organ-song, an echo of the spheric symphony.—And where the air is thinnest and shame melts in the face of the purifying gaze of the near-by sun, there a spirit-structure diamonds itself, matter, making enemies of the senses, matter only to the touchers, deception to the undimmed eye, but to the soul, at home in all the spheres, its very own vesture, and the death of resistances. There the organs turn into miracles, and every eye enfolds, trickles through the body of such a form-dream without hindrance; it contains the synthetically pure man, the creature without blemish and shame and defence.—What is beautiful? Until now we have built as if the earth were doomed to die tomorrow—the ice-death.—An ant spirit has gnawed every child of god down to the skeleton of abstract style. Delight was at home in symmetry and repose; this spirit was latent, seemingly dead or stubborn in the face of an overwhelming god,—or did it sleep in the aeon-ecstasy of its young existence? Now Gulliver awakes and tugs at the countless meshes of Lilliputian snares laid about the sleeping body according to law and equity. The will lives, it seethes, and delight wanders from child's slumber to youth's urge; the extremes are at work; the fires press on; the heavens shout with glee and climb aloft upon the dull, ever and again final deaths;—the midnight sun went to rest at last, and high mounts the radiant globe, since it slept in blackest nights; the revelations of matter breathe, the rigid cramp departed from it, a beneficent drop has awakened the capsules of earth-microbes and vitalises the squatters of millennia-old races,—the delightful mismeasure that engenders the movement is effective once more; we are robbers and cupbearers of the soul; bestowers and poisoners;—the primeval spirit of the Powers lives among us anew. Long live his active race!

The sclerosis of tectonics nears a deliverance. The spirit of the new god of building brooded long over the waters; minutest tentative steps tripped like elfin dances upon the ice of this *terra nova*, and overhead pinioned the Ariel of the holy Utopia and could not discover the valve that might hinder his upward flight towards the fertilizing kiss of his earthly goddess. Yet every new artistic instinct requires human media. To be the interpreter of these lurking forces, to rescue the Gorgon's victims from their age-long curse, granting them a spell of freedom, an hour when spirits walk the earth, for them to re-order their organic elements, this is a most sacred mission and led them to the fate of the builder of the Wassily Blashennoy.

Our European architecture is negative, one-fold, destructive, as befits Hyperboreans, whose homeland is approaching the pole, incomprehensibly slowly, but with incomprehensible certainty, and casting its spectre before it for aeons and aeons. Against this frost-giant the spirit of the earth has brought forth a David, has begotten wish-heroes, which oppose him with a kingdom of engineering and art. Prometheuses, that stole the fire in the hollow cane of their axle-tree. The psyche of man is today more differentiated than the animal species. The religion of the Negative, the angler for pure spirit, may see the goal of human evolution in extreme de-materialization, in the most farreaching simplification, abstraction of the material remnant,—but the antipode will always brace itself to resist this pole, in whose path its Dionysian god has cast the hybrid, the ever more sublime differentiation of spiritualized diversified matter. Everything that is creative in matter belongs to this tribe,—but where the polar opposites flow together and agree to a compromise, there is the resort of the child or the dwarf, the undeveloped or the incompetent. Evolution lies in fragmentation and renewed complication. Monumentalitis, the artless, primary, everything that is given up to enjoyment under the compulsion of mass attraction, is fatigue, sickness, childhood or age. The bridges of sensibility are lacking, that would be capable of reflecting more multifarious complexities also in their complementary, translatory harmony; the entire keyboard is missing, wherewith to receive the polyphonic instrument of such gigantic multiforms.
*Translated by R. A. R.*

# Chronology of buildings and events

**1900**
Death of Friedrich Nietzsche.
Paris Universal Exhibition; success of the *Art Nouveau*.
Antoni Gaudí: Park Güell, Barcelona (1900–14).
Charles Rennie Mackintosh invited to design room for Sezession Exhibition, Vienna.
Hector Guimard: designs for Paris Metro stations.

**1901**
Darmstadt: Exhibition on the Mathildenhöhe. The main building, *Ernst Ludwig Haus* and a number of individual houses by J. M. Olbrich. Peter Behrens designed own house.
Tony Garnier, *Cité industrielle* project.

**1902**
Turin: Applied Art Exhibition. Main buildings by Raimondo D'Aronco in flamboyant *Stile Liberty*.
Van de Velde: Folkwang Museum (remodelling), Hagen, Westphalia.

**1903**
Josef Hoffmann: Purkesdorf Convalescent Home, Vienna (1903–4).
*Wiener Werkstätte* founded, Josef Hoffmann and Koloman Moser leading designers.
Raymond Unwin and B. Parker: First Garden City at Letchworth.
Auguste Perret: Apartment block, 25b Rue Franklin, Paris.
Death of William Morris.
Death of Paul Cézanne.

**1904**
Hermann Muthesius published his three-volume work *Das Englische Haus*.
Giuseppe Terragni born.

**1905**
Otto Wagner: Post Office Savings Bank, Vienna.
Josef Hoffmann: Stoclet House, Brussels.
Frank Lloyd Wright: Larkin Office Building, Buffalo, N.Y.
Antonio Gaudí: Casa Milà, Barcelona (1905–10).
The Dresden *Die Brücke* Group formed, 1905–13.
Einstein's Theory of Relativity.

**1906**
Milan Exhibition.
Palace of Peace Competition, The Hague.
Frank Lloyd Wright: Unity Church, Oak Park.

**1907**
*Deutscher Werkbund* founded by Hermann Muthesius (6 October 1907).
Bruno Paul: Director of School of Arts and Crafts, Berlin.
Unwin and Parker: Hampstead Garden Suburb.
Peter Behrens joined A.E.G.

**1908**
J. M. Olbrich: *Hochzeitsturm* and exhibition buildings, Darmstadt.
H. P. Berlage's book of lectures, *Grundlagen und Entwicklung der Architektur* published.
Publication of *Abstraktion und Einfühlung* by Wilhelm Worringer.

**1908**
Death of J. M. Olbrich.
Mies van der Rohe joined Peter Behrens's Office, 1908–11.
Publication of Adolf Loos's controversial essay 'Ornament and Crime', Vienna.

**1909**
First Garden City in Germany at Hellerau, near Dresden, by Heinrich Tessenow.
Peter Behrens: A.E.G. Turbine Factory, Berlin-Moabit.
R. Östberg: Town Hall, Stockholm.
First Futurist Manifesto from Marinetti appeared in Paris, *Le Figaro*, 29 February.
The foundation of the *Neue Künstlervereinigung* (NKV) at Munich.
Frank Lloyd Wright: Robie House, Chicago.

**1910**
Herwarth Walden's 'Der Sturm' Gallery opened in Berlin. Foundation date of the Expressionist periodical *Der Sturm*.
Adolf Loos: Steiner House, Vienna.
Hans Poelzig: Water Tower, Posen.
Foundation of Austrian *Werkbund*.
Visit of Frank Lloyd Wright to Europe.
Frank Lloyd Wright Exhibition, Berlin. Wasmuth published *Frank Lloyd Wright: Augeführte Bauten und Entwürfe*.
Le Corbusier: visited Germany from Art School at La Chaux-de-Fonds, Switzerland; worked in office of Peter Behrens.

**1911**
Hans Poelzig: Chemical Factory, Luban, 1911–12; Office building, Breslau.
Large Industrial commissions for Peter Behrens from A.E.G.; Germany Embassy building at St Petersburg.
Cubist Exhibition at *Salon des Indépendants*, Paris.
Walter Gropius and Adolf Meyer: Fagus Factory, Alfeld. a.d. Leine (1911–13).
Formation and first Exhibition (Munich, Berlin) of *Der Blaue Reiter*.

**1912**
Futurist Exhibitions in Paris and Berlin.
The publication of Wassily Kandinsky's *Über das Geistige in der Kunst* ('Concerning the spiritual in art').

**1913**
Bruno Taut: Steel Industries Pavilion, Leipzig Fair.
*Jahrhundertfeier*, Breslau, opening of the Centenary Hall designed by Max Berg.
Swiss *Werkbund* founded.
*Het Scheepvaarthuis* built in Amsterdam by van der Meij (1913–16).
Michel de Klerk: *Eigen Haard* Housing Scheme, Spaarndammerplantsoen, Amsterdam.
Rudolf Steiner's Goetheanum I, opened at Dornach, Switzerland.
Guillaume Apollinaire's book *Les peintres cubistes* published.

**1914**
Outbreak of First World War (1914–18).
*Deutscher Werkbund* Cologne Exhibition. Model Theatre by Henri van de Velde; Model Factory by Walter Gropius and Adolf Meyer; Glass Pavilion by Bruno Taut.
Paul Scheerbart published his book *Glasarchitektur*, Berlin.
Antonio Sant'Elia: Manifesto of Futurist Architecture.
Le Corbusier: Dom-Ino house project.

**1915**
Death of Paul Scheerbart.
Tony Garnier: Lyon Stadium.
Foundation of Design and Industries Association, London. Modelled on the *Deutscher Werkbund*.

**1916**
*Werkbund* competition: House of Friendship, Constantinople.
Le Corbusier: Villa at La Chaux-de-Fonds.
Robert van 't Hoff: Huis ter Heide projects, Holland.
Franz Marc killed at Verdun.

**1917**
Foundation of *de Stijl* group at Leiden, Holland.
De Klerk began the extension of the *Eigen Haard*
Estate along the Zaanstraat.
Death of Antonio Sant'Elia.
Frank Lloyd Wright: Imperial Hotel, Tokio.

**1918**
*Novembergruppe* and the *Arbeitsrat für Kunst* formed
in Berlin.
Bruno Taut: Architectural Programme for the
*Arbeitsrat für Kunst*.
J. J. P. Oud: appointed City Architect of Rotterdam.
Le Corbusier and Ozenfant publish *Après le cubisme*.
*Wendingen* first published by *Architectura et Amicitia*
in Amsterdam.
1st *de Stijl* Group Manifesto, Leiden.

**1919**
Gropius reorganized the Weimar Academy of Fine
Art and Arts and Crafts School; restyled under the
title *Das Staatliche Bauhaus, Weimar*. 1st *Bauhaus*
Manifesto.
Mies van der Rohe: glass skyscraper and office
projects (1919–22)
Erich Mendelsohn opens Berlin office. Exhibition of
sketches, 'Architecture in Steel and Glass' at
Cassirer's Berlin Gallery.
*Arbeitsrat für Kunst* exhibition for 'Unknown
Architects', Berlin.
Hans Poelzig: *Grosses Schauspielhaus*, Berlin, opened.
The 'Utopian Correspondence' of the *Gläserne
Kette* (1919–20).
Friedrichstrasse Competition, Berlin.
Bruno Taut: published *Alpine Architektur*, Hagen, and
*Die Stadtkrone*, Jena.

**1920**
Bruno Taut: Berlin editions of *Frühlicht* (January–
July 1920). Published *Die Auflösung der Städte*, Hagen,
and *Der Welt-baumeister*, Hagen.
Rudolf Wiene's film *The Cabinet of Dr Caligari*
(1920–1).
Hans Poelzig: Salzburg *Festspielhaus* project (1st
study), 1920–1.

**1920**
Le Corbusier founded the revue *L'Esprit nouveau* with
Ozenfant and Dermée.
Michel de Klerk: houses on the Henriette Ronner-
plein, Amsterdam, 1920–2.

**1921**
Erich Mendelsohn: Completion of Einstein Tower,
Potsdam; *Berliner Tageblatt* building (for Rudolf
Mosse), 1921–3 (built in collaboration with Richard
Neutra and sculptor R. P. Henning).
Bruno Taut: appointed *Stadtbaurat* (City Planning
Officer), Magdeburg, 1921. Published new series of
*Frühlicht* from Magdeburg, 1921–2.
Otto Bartning: *Sternkirche* project.
Piet Kramer: *De Dageraad* Estate, Amsterdam,
1921–3 (projected 1918).

**1922**
Van Doesburg visited the *Bauhaus* at Weimar.
Chicago Tribune Tower Competition.
J. J. P. Oud: the Oud Mathenese Estate, Rotterdam.
Hans Poelzig: revised schemes for the Salzburg
*Festspielhaus*.
Walter Gropius: Town Theatre, Jena.
First exhibition of the *Berliner Sezession*, 1922–3.

**1923**
Fritz Höger: *Chilehaus*, Hamburg.
The publication of Le Corbusier's *Vers une architec-
ture* in Paris.
Completion of Erich Mendelsohn's Luckenwalde
Factory.
Hugo Häring: Gut Garkau Farm buildings, 1923–4.
Death of Michel de Klerk.

**1924**
Formation of the Berlin 'Circle of Ten' (*Zehner
Ring*), 1923–4.
Arthur Korn made Secretary of the *Novembergruppe*.
Gerrit Rietveld: Schröder House at Utrecht.
Surrealist manifesto (Breton).

**1925**

*Bauhaus* moved to Dassau. New buildings by Walter Gropius (1925–6).
Formation of the Berlin 'Ring' basically from the original 'Circle of Ten'.
Le Corbusier: Pavilion '*l'Esprit Nouveau*', at Paris Exhibition. Publication of *Urbanisme*.
Peter Behrens's house 'New Ways' at Northampton (1925–6).
Reconstruction of *Unter den Linden*, Berlin. Prize winners: C. van Eesteren and T. van Doesburg.
Death of Adolf Meyer.
Death of Rudolf Steiner.

**1926**

Publication of German Edition of Le Corbusier's *Vers une Architecture* (*Kommende Baukunst*).
Adolf Loos: House for Tristan Tzara, Paris.
Ernst May: plans for Frankfurt-am-Main.
Death of Antonio Gaudí.
Mies van der Rohe: Monument to Karl Liebknecht and Rosa Luxemburg, Berlin.

**1927**

*Werkbund* Exhibition at Weissenhofsiedlung, Stuttgart. Director: Mies van der Rohe.
Walter Gropius: Total Theatre project.
Buckminster Fuller's Dymaxion House project.
Brinkmann, Van de Vlugt and Stam: the Van Nelle Factory, Rotterdam.
Publication of Gustav Platz's *Die Baukunst der Neuesten Zeit*, Berlin.
Publication of K. Malevitch's *Die gegendstandlose Welt* in German (Bauhaus Book no. 11).
Publication of Le Corbusier's book *Vers une architecture* in an English translation, *Towards a new architecture*.

**1927**

Death of Hermann Obrist.
Death of Hermann Muthesius.

**1928**

Formation of C.I.A.M. at La Sarraz.
Le Corbusier, Villa Savoye, Poissy; Centrosoyus, Moscow project.
Walter Gropius leaves *Bauhaus*; Hannes Meyer appointed Director.
Erich Mendelsohn: Schocken Store, Chemnitz.
First Rationalist Architects' Exhibition, Rome.
Publication of Moholy Nagy's *Von Material zur Architektur*.
Death of Charles Rennie Mackintosh in London.
Goetheanum II at Dornach opened.
W. M. Dudok: Town Hall, Hilversum, 1928–30.

**1929**

Mies van der Rohe: *Werkbund* Pavilion, Barcelona Exhibition.
Walter Gropius: Housing, Berlin-Siemenstadt.
Richard Neutra: Lovell House, California, U.S.A.
Second C.I.A.M. conference at Frankfurt-am-Main.
B. Bijvoet and J. Duiker: *Zonnestraal* Sanatorium, Hilversum.
Bruno Taut published *Modern architecture* (German and English editions).

**1930**

Mies van der Rohe appointed Director of the *Bauhaus*, 1930–3.
*Deutscher Werkbund* Pavilion at Paris Exhibition designed by Walter Gropius and Marcel Breuer.
Le Corbusier: Swiss Pavilion, Paris University.
Karl Marx Hof, Vienna.

# Bibliography

## General References on modern architecture

| | |
|---|---|
| Banham, R. | *Theory and design in the first Machine Age.* London, 1960. |
| | *Guide to modern architecture.* London, 1962. |
| Behne, A. | *Die moderne Zweckbau.* Munich, 1926. (Republished 1964 by Ullstein, Berlin) |
| Blake, P. | *The master builders.* London, 1960 |
| Blijstra, R. | *Netherlands architecture since 1900.* Amsterdam, 1960 |
| Cassou, J., Langui, E., and Pevsner, N. | *The sources of modern art.* London, 1962 |
| Pehnt, W., ed. | *Encyclopaedia of modern architecture.* London, 1963 |
| Hitchcock, H-R. | *Modern architecture: romanticism and reintegration.* New York, 1929 |
| | *Architecture: nineteenth and twentieth centuries.* Harmondsworth, 1958 |
| Hoffmann, H. | *New German architecture.* London, 1956 |
| Howarth, T. | *Charles Rennie Mackintosh and the modern movement.* London, 1952 |
| Jaffé, H. L. C. | *De Stijl: 1917–1931. The Dutch contribution to modern art.* London, 1953 |
| Joedicke, J. | *A history of modern architecture.* London, 1960 |
| Le Corbusier | *Vers une architecture.* Paris, 1923. (Translation: *Towards a new architecture.* London, 1927) |
| Madsen, S. T. | *Sources of Art Nouveau.* Oslo, 1956 |
| McGrath, R. | *Twentieth century houses.* London, 1934 |
| Muthesius, H. | *Das Englische Haus.* 3 vols. Berlin, 1904 |
| Onderdonk, T. S. | *The ferro-concrete style.* New York, 1928 |
| Pevsner, N. | *Pioneers of modern design.* London, 1936. (Pelican edition, 1960) |
| | *An outline of European architecture.* London, 1942. (Pelican, 7th edition 1963: Pelican Jubilee edition 1961) |
| Platz, G. A. | *Die Baukunst der neuesten Zeit.* Berlin, 1927 |
| Richards, J. M. | *An introduction to modern architecture.* Harmondsworth, 1940 (Pelican). (Re-issued in 1961 by Cassell, London, in hardback form) |

| Schmutzler, R. | *Art Nouveau*. London, 1964 |
| Taut, B. | *Modern architecture*. London, 1929 |
| Vriend, J. J. | *Nieuwere architectuur*. Bussum, 1957 |
| Wattjes, J. G. | *Modern Dutch architecture*. London, 1928 |
| Whittick, A. | *European architecture of the twentieth century*. 2 vols. London, 1950–3 |
| Zevi, B. | *Towards an organic architecture*. London, 1949 |
| | *Storia dell'architettura*. Milan, 1950 (1955) |
| | *Architecture as space*. New York, 1957 |

## Visionary, Expressionistic and Fantastic architecture

This section does not include any of the volumes listed later under 'Monographs'; it should be used in conjunction with that section.

| Banham, R. | 'The glass paradise', *Architectural Review*, February 1959, pp. 87–90. (A discussion of the ideas and work of Scheerbart the writer and Taut the architect) |
| Behne, A. | 'Hollandische Baukunst in der Gegenwart, *Wasmuth's Monatshefte für Baukunst*, Year 6, 1921–2, pp. 1–32. |
| | 'De Duitsche Torenhuis Bouw', *Wendingen*, no. 3, 1923, p. 15ff. |
| Beyer, O. | 'Architectuur in Ijzer en Beton', *Wendingen*, no. 10, 1920. (Special issue on Mendelsohn) |
| Conrads, U. and Sperlich, H. G. | *Fantastic architecture*. London, 1963. Translated and expanded from the original German edition (Stuttgart, 1960) by C. C. and G. R. Collins. (A wide ranging survey important for its inclusion of the Architectural Programme of the *Arbeitsrat für Kunst* and extracts from the writings of Taut, Scheerbart, Finsterlin, Behne, etc.) See also article culled from this book in *Zodiac*, no. 5, 1957, pp. 117–31 |
| Conrads, U., ed. | 'Berlin: Dokumente europäischen Bauens', *Bauwelt*, nos. 41–2, October 1961. (A special issue of the magazine devoted to a photographic record of building in Berlin from the beginning of this century; includes contemporary documents) |
| Gregotti, V. | 'L'architettura dell'expressionismo', *Casabella*, no. 254, pp. 24–50. (Illustrated with 108 photographs, many of which are relevant to the text) |
| | 'Peter Behrens: 1868–1940', *Casabella*, no. 240, pp. 5–8. (Leading article in the edition devoted to Behrens's work) |
| Hajos, E. M., and Zahn, L. | *Berliner Architektur der Nachkriegszeit*. Berlin, 1928 |
| Lindahl, G. | 'Von der Zukunftskathedrale bis zur Wohnmaschine', in *Idea and form*, Stockholm, 1959, pp. 226–82. (An important essay in which Taut's *Glashaus* is discussed in detail as well as the activities of the Utopian groups) |

| Müller-Wulckow, W. | *Aufbau-Architektur!* Berlin, 1919. In the series *Tribune der Kunst und Zeit* (edited by Kasimir Edschmid) |
| Rave, R., and | *Bauen seit 1900: Ein Führer durch Berlin.* Berlin, 1963 |
| Knöfel, H. J. | 'Modern Dutch architecture', *Architectural Review*, August 1922, pp. 46–50. (The work of Michel de Klerk) |
| Robertson, H. | 'Modern Dutch architecture', *Architectural Review*, March 1923, pp. 97–101. (Kramer and Dudok) |
| Staal, J. F. | 'Bouwerk van Vorkink en Wormser', *Wendingen*, no. 6, 1921 |
| Wijdeveld, H. Th. | 'Het Park Meerwijk te Bergen', *Wendingen*, no. 8, 1918, pp. 3 ff. |
| | 'Architectonische Phantasien in de wereld der Kristallen', *Wendingen*, no. 12, 1924, pp. 3 ff. |

## General references on painting, literature, drama and the background to the Expressionist movement

| Barr, A. | *Masters of modern art.* New York, 1954 |
| Barr, H. | *Expressionismus.* Munich, 1926 (London, 1925) |
| Benesch, O. | *Edvard Munch.* London, 1960 |
| Bithell, J. | *Modern German literature.* London, 1936 |
| Buchheim, L-G. | *Der blauer Reiter.* Feldafing, 1959 |
| Craig, E. G. | *On the art of the theatre.* London, 1911 (paperback, 1962) |
| Frenzel, H. A., and E. | *Daten deutscher Dichtung Chronologischer Abriss der deutschen Literaturgeschichte.* Band II: *Vom Biedermeier bis zur Gegenwart*, 1953 (paperback, 1962) |
| Garten, H. F. | *Modern German drama.* London, 1959 |
| Gray, R. | *Brecht.* London, 1961 |
| Grohmann, W. | *Paul Klee,* London, 1954 |
| Haftmann, W. | *Painting in the twentieth century.* 2 vols. London, 1960 (paperback 1965). (Probably the best introduction to painting available, with a bias towards the German contribution. Vol. 1, text; Vol. 2, illustrations) |
| Hamburger, M. | *Reason and energy.* London, 1957. (See particularly Chapter VI) |
| Hess, H. | *Dank in Farben.* Munich, 1957. (A small anecdotal volume providing a glimpse of the character of some of the Expressionist artists) |
| | *Lyonel Feininger.* London, 1961 |
| Hoffmann, E. | *Expressionism.* London, 1957. (A small but useful introduction to the Expressionist painters. 64 pp.) |
| Kafka, F. | *The castle.* Harmondsworth (Penguin), 1953 |
| | *The trial.* Harmondsworth (Penguin), 1955 |

| | |
|---|---|
| Kandinsky, W. | *Über das Geistige in der Kunst*. Munich, 1911. (English edition *On the spiritual in art*. New York, 1946) |
| Kracauer, S. | *From Caligari to Hitler: A psychological history of the German film*. London, 1947 |
| Lake, L., and Maillard, R., eds. | *A dictionary of modern painting*. London, 1958 |
| Landsberger, F. | *Impressionismus und Expressionismus*. Leipzig, 1919 |
| Lissitzky, E., and Arp, H. | *Die Kunstismen*. Zürich, 1925 |
| Myers, B. S. | *Expressionism*. London, 1957. (A thorough exploration of Expressionism in painting and the related arts.) A concise edition, *Expressionism: A generation in revolt*. London, 1963 |
| Nietzsche, F. | *Die Geburt der Trageodie aus dem Geiste der Musik*. Leipzig, 1872. English translation in *The birth of tragedy and the genealogy of morals*. New York, 1956 *The authorized English translation of Nietzsche's works*. Translated by Oscar Levy, 18 volumes, 1909–13 *Thus Spoke Zarathustra*. Harmondsworth, 1961. Introduction and translation by R. J. Hollingdale |
| Read, H. | *Art now*. London, 1933 (paperback, 1961). (See Part III) *A concise history of modern painting*. London, 1959 |
| Reinhardt, K. F. | 'The Expressionist Movement in recent German literature', *The Germanic Review*. Vol. VI, 1931. New York (Columbia University), pp. 256–65 |
| Samuel, R., and Thomas, R. H. | *Expressionism in German art, life, literature and the theatre*. Cambridge, 1936. (An excellent comprehensive survey from the English point of view) |
| Seuphor, M., ed. | *A dictionary of abstract painting*. London, 1957 |
| Soergel, A. | *Dichtung und Dichter der Zeit*. 2 vols., Leipzig, 1925. (The classic literary history of Expressionism) |
| Sokel, W. H. | *The writer in extremis: Expressionism in twentieth century German literature*. California (Stanford University Press), 1959. |
| Strindberg, A. | *Three plays*. Harmondsworth (Penguin), 1958. Translated by P. Watts. *Eight Expressionist plays*. New York, 1965. Translated by A. Paulson with an introduction by J. Gassner |
| Theone, P. (pseud.) | *Modern German art*. Harmondsworth (Pelican Special), 1938 |
| von Sydow, E. | *Die deutsche expressionistische Kultur und Malerie*. Berlin, 1920. (An Expressionist apology) |
| Walden, H. | *Die neue Malerie*. 2nd edn. Berlin, 1919 |
| Wingler, H. M. | *Das Bauhaus: 1919–1937 Weimar, Dessau, Berlin*. Bransche, 1962 |
| Worringer, W. | *Abstraktion und Einfühlung*. Munich, 1908. English translation *Abstraction and empathy: A contribution to the psychology of style*. London, 1953 |

## Monographs

Included in this part of the bibliography are a brief selection of books and magazine articles that show representative examples of the work of individual architects. For a wider and more detailed list see the author's 'The Modern Movement in architecture; a biographical bibliography', supplement to the *Architectural Association Journal*, December 1963 and *Sources of Modern Architecture; A bibliography*, London, 1966

*Behrens, Peter*

Hoeber, F.        *Peter Behrens*. Munich, 1913

Cremers, P. J.        *Peter Behrens, sein Werk von 1909 bis zur Gegenwart*. Essen, 1928

Misc.        'Peter Behrens'. *Casabella*, no. 240. (Special issue)

*Finsterlin, Hermann*

Finsterlin, H.        'Finsterlin: Vormenspel in de Architectuur', *Wendingen*, no. 3, 1924. (Special issue)

'Der achte Tag', *Frühlicht*, no. 11, 1920

'Innenarchitektur', *Frühlicht*, Winter 1921–2

'Die Genesis der Weltarchitektur oder die Deszendenz der Dome als Stilspiel', *Frühlicht*, Spring 1923. (All these articles from *Frühlicht* are reproduced in B. Taut, ed., *Frühlicht 1920–22*. Berlin, 1963)

Pevsner, N.        'Finsterlin and some others', *Architectural Review*, November 1962, pp. 353–7

See also bibliographical section: 'Exhibition catalogues'

*Gaudí, Antonio*

Collins, G. R.        *Antonio Gaudí*, London, 1960. (An admirable study with full bibliography, pp. 131–4)

Sert, J. L., and Sweeny J.        *Antonio Gaudí*. London, 1960

*Gropius, Walter*

Gropius, Walter        *Idee und Aufbau des Staatlichen Bauhauses*. Munich, 1923

*Internationale Architektur*. Munich, 1925 (reprinted 1965). Bauhaus Book no. 1

*Neue Arbeiten der Bauhaus-werkstätten*. Munich, 1926. Bauhaus Book, no. 7

*Bauhausbauten Dessau*. Munich, 1930. Bauhaus Book no. 12

*The New Architecture and the Bauhaus*. London, 1935 (paperback 1964). Translated by P. Morton Shand

Giedion, S.        *Walter Gropius*. Paris, 1931 (paperback)

*Walter Gropius*. London, 1954

Scheffauer, H. G.        'The work of Walter Gropius', *Architectural Review*, August 1924, pp. 50–4

*Häring, Hugo*

Lauterbach, H., and Joedicke, J. — *Hugo Haering: Schriften, Entwürfe, Bauten.* Stuttgart, 1965

Joedicke, J. — 'Haering at Garkau', *Architectural Review*, May 1960, pp. 313–8

'Hugo Haering: Zur Theorie des Organheften Bauen', *Bauen und Wohnen*, no. 11, 1960, pp. 419 ff.

*Hoetger, Bernhard*

Uphoff, C. E. — *Bernhard Hoetger.* Leipzig, 1919. ('Junge Kunst', Band 3)

*Klerk, Michel de*

Staal, F. — Michel de Klerk, 'Onuitgevoerde ontwerpen', *Wendingen*, no. 4–5, 1924

Kramer, P. — 'De Bouwwerken van Michel de Klerk', *Wendingen*, no. 9–10, 1924

*Korn, Arthur*

Korn, Arthur — 'Analytische und Utopische Architektur', *Das Kunstblatt*, vol. 11–12, 1923. Reprinted in U. Conrads, *Programme und Manifeste zur Architektur des 20 Jahrhunderts.* Berlin, 1964. pp. 71–2

*Glas im Bau und als Gebrauchsgegenstand.* Berlin, 1929. (An important book on the new glass buildings in Berlin)

Housden, B., ed. — 'Arthur Korn'. *Architectural Association Journal*, December 1957. (Special issue)

*Krayl, Carl*

Konrad, G. E. — *Maxim Worm – Carl Krayl, Architekten Magdeburg.* Berlin, Vienna, n.d.

*Kreis, Wilhelm*

Mayer, H. K. F., and Rehder, G. — *Wilhelm Kreis.* Essen, 1953

*Luckhardt, Wassili and Hans*

Kultermann, U. — *Wassili und Hans Luckhardt: Bauten und Entwürfe*, Tübingen, 1958

*Mendelsohn, Erich*

Mendelsohn, E. — 'Erich Mendelsohn: Bauten und Skizzen', *Wasmuth's Monatshefte für Baukunst*, year 8, 1924. pp. 3–66. English reprint, 'Erich Mendelsohn: structures and sketches', London, 1924 (translated by H. G. Scheffauer).

*Das Gesamtschaffen des Architekten, Skizzen, Entwürfe, Bauten.* Berlin, 1930

*Briefe eines Architekten.* Munich, 1961. (A selection of the letters written by Mendelsohn to his wife from 1910 to 1953.) Edited by Oskar Beyer

Whittick, A. — *Erich Mendelsohn.* London, 1940. (3rd edn. 1965)

Beyer, O. — 'Architectuur in Ijzer en Beton', *Wendingen*, no. 10, 1920. (Special issue showing a number of Mendelsohn's early sketches)

Banham, R. — 'Mendelsohn', *Architectural Review.* August, 1954, pp. 85–93

Misc. — 'Erich Mendelsohn', *Architectural Forum.* April, 1953, pp. 105–21

| | |
|---|---|
| Misc. | 'Erich Mendelsohn', *L'Architettura*, no. 95, September 1963. (Special issue with articles by Bruno Zevi and Louise Mendelsohn. The complete series of Mendelsohn sketches appeared in *L'Architettura*, 1963–4) |
| *Poelzig, Hans* | |
| Heuss, T. | *Hans Poelzig: Lebensbild eines Baumeisters*. Tübingen, 1939 (1955) |
| | *Hans Poelzig: Bauten und Entwürfe*. Berlin, 1939 |
| Scheffauer, H. G. | 'Hans Poelzig', *Architectural Review*, October 1923, pp. 122–7 |
| Posener, J. | 'Poelzig', *Architectural Review*. June 1963, pp. 401–5 |
| *Scharoun, Hans* | |
| Scharoun, Hans | 'Raum und Milieu der Schule', *Bauen und Wohnen*, no. 4, 1961, pp. 4–8 |
| Staber, M. | 'Hans Scharoun: a contribution to organic building', 1961, *Zodiac* 10, pp. 53–78 |
| *Scheerbart, Paul* | |
| Scheerbart, P. | *Glasarchitektur*. Berlin, 1914 |
| | 'Glashausbriefe', *Frühlicht*, 1920 |
| | 'Die Architektenkongress: eine Parlamentsgeschichte', *Frühlicht*, Autumn 1921. (The last two articles are reproduced in B. Taut, *Frühlicht 1920–22*. Berlin, 1963) |
| *Steiner, Rudolf* | |
| Steiner, R. | *The story of my life*. London, 1928 |
| | *Architectural forms considered as the thoughts of culture and world perception*. London, 1919 |
| | *Ways to a new style in architecture*. London and New York, 1928 |
| | *Der Baugedanke des Goetheanum*. Stuttgart, 1932 (1958) |
| Harwood, A. C., ed. | *The faithful thinker*. London, 1961. (See essay by K. Bayes. 'Architecture in Accord with Man', pp. 163–78) |
| Sharp, D. | 'Rudolf Steiner and the way to a new style in architecture', *Architectural Association Journal*. June 1963, pp. 371–83 |
| *Taut, Bruno* | |
| Taut, B. | *Alpine Architektur*. Hagen, 1919 |
| | *Die Stadtkrone*. Jena, 1919. (Including essays by Scheerbart, Baron and Behne) |
| | *Der Weltbaumeister*. Hagen and Munich, 1920 |
| | *Die Auflösung der Städte, oder die Erde eine gute Wohnung*. Hagen and Munich, 1920 |
| | *Frühlicht*. Magdeburg, 1921–2, 4 editions. (The earlier editions of *Frühlicht* appeared as supplements to *Stadtbaukunst alter und neuer Zeit*, 1920–1. All the issues have been reproduced in B. Taut, *Frühlicht: Eine Folge für die Verwirklichung des neuen Baugedankens*. Berlin, 1963. (Edited by U. Conrads) |
| | *Die neue Wohnung*. Leipzig, 1924 |
| | *Bauen: Der neue Wohnbau*. 1927 |
| | *Modern architecture*. London, 1929 |

| | |
|---|---|
| Taut, B. | 'The nature and aims of architecture', *The Studio*, March 1929, pp. 170–4 |
| Scheffauer, H. G. | 'Bruno Taut: a visionary in practice', *Architectural Review*, December 1922, pp. 155–9 |
| *Van de Velde, Henri* | |
| Van de Velde, H. | *Der neue Stil*. Weimar, 1906 |
| | *Vom neuen Stil*. Leipzig, 1907 |
| | *Les formules de la beauté architectonique moderne*. Brussels, 1923 |
| | *Le théâtre de l'exposition du 'Werkbund' à Cologne, 1914 et la scène tripartite*. Antwerp, 1925 |
| | *Geschichte meines Lebens*. Munich, 1962 |
| Osthaus, K. E. | *Van de Velde*. Hagen, 1920 |
| Shand, P. M. | 'Van de Velde to Wagner', *Architectural Review*, October 1934, pp. 131–4 |
| Misc. | 'Numero dedicato ad Henry van de Velde', *Casabella*, no. 237 |

*Exhibition Catalogues*

*Um 1900*. Kunstgewerbemuseum. Zürich, 1953

*A hundred years of German painting*. Tate Gallery. London, 1956

*Les sources du XXe siècle*. Musée National d'Art Moderne. Paris, 1960

*Expressionismus: Literatur und Kunst, 1910–23*. Schiller-Nationalmuseum. Marbach (Munich), 1960

*Polariteit: het Appolinische en het Dionysische in de Kunst*. Stedelijk Museum. Amsterdam, 1961

*Kokoshka*. Tate Gallery, London, 1962

*Sketches by Erich Mendelsohn*. R.I.B.A. London, 1962

*Die Gläserne Kette: Visionäre Architekturen aus dem Kreis um Bruno Taut, 1919–1920*. Museum Leverkusen and Akademie der Künste. Berlin, 1963

*60 Jahre Finsterlin: Querschnitt durch sein Schaffen*. Munich, 1964

*L'Espressionismo: pittura, scultura, architettura*. Palazzo Strozzi, Florence, 1964. (Vallecchi Editore)

*Max Taut*. Akademie der Künste. Berlin, 1964

*Poelzig, Endell, Moll und die Breslauer Kunstakademie*. Akademie der Künste. Berlin, 1965

# Index